AVERAGE TO ABUNDANT

HOW ORDINARY PEOPLE BUILD SUSTAINABLE
WEALTH AND ENJOY THE PROCESS

BY
LUCAS D. SHALLUA

Printed in the United States of America

First Printing, January 2020

ISBN 978-1-734-3849-0-1

ISBN 9781734384901

51995 >

9 781734 384901

Global Empowerment Press
6000 Museum Drive
Winston Salem, NC 27105
USA

www.Globalempowermentpress.com

TABLE OF CONTENT

Acknowledgements

To my beautiful wife, great partner and best friend Dr. Dorothy Shallua, who has been encouraging me throughout the process. And my lovely kids Emmy, Joshua, Dora and David! To my lovely Mom and always wise Dad—

Foreword

I'm glad that Dr. Lucas D. Shallua has been able to answer the question why the simple remain in poverty while the wise build wealth on a daily basis. Average to Abundant is a written in a simple and practical way for average people regardless of their background and locality to systematically start the journey towards abundant life. This book will help you to demystify poverty and enable you to use the unlimited power within you to overcome every element of poverty in your live. Average to Abundant shares in details the universal principles of wealth generation and successful living available to everyone as originally intended by the creator. It is one thing to learn and accumulate head knowledge and completely another thing to put in action all that has been learned. The challenge is to work on baby steps to implement all the principles you have learned and make wealth a reality in your life.

—Anthony Luvanda
Speaker, Trainer, Entrepreneur

Introduction

Wealth and poverty are both a mental state. It is not abundance or scarcity of resources, but in principle a *belief system*. If we can alter how we *think, act* and *see* the world around us; then we can easily change our state of affairs.

If you are considering professions to help you get wealthy, many high-paying conventional and traditional jobs might tempt you. I trained as a veterinary surgeon and doctor; practiced and then taught at a university level but that did not suffice in the quest of building personal wealth. Principles, insight and steps shared in this book helped me personally to systematically change my mindset from poverty to wealth; and as an immigrant to USA— in less than 15 years, my wife Dorothy and I were able to cross the million-dollar mark net worth.

The reason I wrote this books is simply to answer the question asked so many times by those who hear our story, and probably you are asking the same question— How come that you landed in USA empty-handed, worked the lowest-paying jobs and in a short period of time you have realized the American dream?

Every chapter in this book is an attempt to answer that question in a very practical and simple way that we personally followed and the experiences from other success achievers that cement the ideas that we value and hold dear to our hearts. We are still students learning and the things we have proven to work we share them freely to the world. *Freely we have been given and freely we give;* is our mantra and our ultimate joy is to hear testimonials of people who have achieved greater goals through inspiration from our story and the insight shared here!

In this book the goal is to take you through that process and quickly put you in the driver's seat to take control of your life to start creating wealth. The process is simple; first we'll attempt to clear the misconception about wealth by differentiating it from riches. Many people miss the mark very early by pursuing the wrong thing and poorly defining their goal. A wise personal performance trainer once said, "if you do not know where you are going then any road will take you there". The journey of building wealth is not free from woes and pitfalls for those who are not careful and previously warned. Reckless traveling on this path has left many wounded, traumatized and arrived with lots of scars, loss and others do not make it to the finish line at all. Most emphasis is put on the journey itself; on how to enjoy life while building wealth and leading a balanced and enriched life.

Important principles of generating wealth, practical steps, underlining wisdom and experiences from other successful achievers have been carefully presented for you to sit back and learn in simple terms on how to get started, what are dos and don'ts of the journey. Most examples are from our personal experiences in this route from our own failures, successes and mistakes for you to learn. My mother was a story teller; I take pleasure in retelling her bedtime or kitchen stories and use the moral of these stories to bring the point across.

Average to Abundant is a unique book compared to other millions of wealth generating books out there because it uses simple terms and principles that are practicable to ordinary people that are non-professional in the world of finances and business. Facts, principles, and wisdom are presented as they are —in simple language that anybody can understand. I have read hundreds of finance and wealth books so far and my biggest problem is the concepts are hard to understand and the language used is difficult—bear in mind I am a veterinary surgeon, professor and multilingual, I do not consider myself dumb by any standard.

The benefit of reading this book is transformation to wealth mindset that puts you on a super highway to building personal wealth, improved wellbeing and disciplined lifestyle that is admired by many. The chapters of this book will address the fundamental questions of wealth creation; that is *what, how, where, when, who* and *which.*

one

WEALTHY —MEANING

"The real measure of your wealth is how much you'd be worth if you lost all your money..."

—Anonymous

In the kitchen as a little boy, the only thing that would motivate me to be there and help my mother with dish preparation was her stories that were deep in meaning at the same time entertaining. This story of the rich woman's ring got stuck in my head for many years and it still resonates with me as if it was told yesterday. As she taught me how to remove the scales of the fish in the kitchen sink, she pulled her chair across the kitchen and started the tale of three people who were in deep argument standing on the bridge.

The debate was centered on the fact that once you have the success secret and ingredients; then you can never be poor again in your life and money is everything and should be pursued at any cost. It was in the cold winters where the chilly wind was blowing hard and the rich woman covered herself with very expensive fur coat, boots and wore a golden signet ring that symbolizes riches that she deserved because of her hard work and business intelligence. She insisted during the debate with other two casual gentlemen who were her acquaintances that she will never ever be broke again in her life, does not need anything or anybody because she inevitably had discovered the recipe for riches and she magnetizes opportunities with no effort. To make her point; she took off her expensive golden signet ring from the finger, held it on her hand and declared boldly saying, *"if this ring returns back to me then I will know that I can again be poor and broke, but otherwise it will never happen in my life again."*After that declaration and proclamation she tossed the ring in the ocean and rested her case.

Few years went by and she was preparing a special dinner for the guests who were visiting with her that night. As she was cleaning and eviscerating one of the fish she got from the fish market a big surprise was waiting for her; an expensive, sparkling, golden signet ring! She was so excited and couldn't wait to tell her special guests how lucky she was to get such an expensive ring in the belly of the fish! As she was telling the story to her guests during dinner, one of the guests reminded her that the signet ring belonged to her in the past; and that she tossed it in the ocean many years ago with the declaration attached to it during a debate around riches. As they were still at the dinner table talking and dining together, a phone rang and she was informed that her truck that was carrying the merchandise for her shops was involved in an accident and villagers looted all the goods.

As she was trying to comprehend what has happened, there was a knock at the door, two policemen were there to deliver sad news about her supermarket that had burned down to ashes and firemen couldn't put out the fire or rescue anything. While the policemen were still there; another phone rang yet another bad news of a ship that sank with all her merchandize. That ended up being the longest night of her life and by the morning all the riches she had disappeared in one day! She sat down on the floor after long and sleepless hours of the night crying and she looked towards heaven and declared; *"Now I know, surely money can be gone in a flash, as if it had grown wings and flown away like an eagle!"*

One of the most debated and talked about issues in our society today is riches and wealth. The vast majority of people believe that to be wealthy, you must become rich by accumulating large sums of money. Some believe being wealthy is a result of hard work and sacrifice. Others believe being wealthy is a result of taking advantage of someone else.

Some religious and faith-based groups hold a belief that if you are not wealthy, you are missing out on what "God" or "Superior Being" wants for you. With all of these perspectives, we should seek to know the true meaning of wealth in a more balanced and logical manner.

Wealth is a mindset; what you know and your perspective of life will determine your net worth. If you want to be wealthy, you'll need to think like the wealthy. Start by defining your goals in a year's time and then five years' time. Wealth mindset matters and is crucial at this time and era because 60% of Americans live paycheck to paycheck and it only gets worse when we consider the rising levels of credit card debt. These behaviors create vicious cyclones of debt and dependence from which it is difficult to escape.

It seems that the ability to attain wealth; which is the basics of the wealth mindset is a lost art. A mindset is a lens through which we view the world. Like a pair of sunglasses, it can slightly alter what you see and how you think about it. Mindsets are comprised of *beliefs, perceptions, and attitudes* that inform our thoughts and decisions. Different mindsets are an important part of our toolkit for success, like glasses, they can obscure our path or bring clarity to the road ahead. Cultivating a healthy wealth mindset will help us develop new goals and find ways to increase our potential to create sustainable wealth that can spin through generations. If we dig deeper into the stories of wealthy people, we will notice a pattern. Rarely will a wealthy person be able to boil down their success to a single miraculous moment. Instead, they will cite their mindset as the biggest reason for their prosperity. A wealth mindset is a set of *beliefs, habits, and behaviors* that separates the wealthy from the rest. A wealth mindset will guide us to make the most of the wealth we have. But it doesn't come easy as it means spending less, making wise decisions, and looking for ways to improve with minimal risk. The good news is that with a little dedication, anyone can develop this mindset.

The antithesis of a wealth mindset is a poor mindset. Most who have this *"poor mindset"* or *"poverty mentality"* don't even realize they have it. A poor mindset generates the thinking that attaining wealth is impossible, that it can be done without effort, or that one just does not have the special sauce it takes to become wealthy. This mindset undermines our goals and will actively drive wealth away from us unless we work to counteract it. Very few wealthy people became rich overnight; building wealth is a slow and steady process.

Facebook didn't turn Mark Zuckerberg into a billionaire; he created it with his hard work and dedication, and then reaped the benefits of his labor when the time was ripe.

> *The average wealthy person spends 10 times more time planning their finances than the average middle-class individual.*
> *—Thomas J. Stanley, "The Millionaire Next Door"*

What is Wealth?

Since people's opinions vary so much today on the definition of wealth, an historic definition of wealth needs to be made. Webster's 1828 Dictionary defines wealth as follows (1): "WEALTH, n. 1. Prosperity; external happiness. 2. Riches; large possessions of money, goods, or land; that abundance of worldly estate which exceeds the estate of the greater part of the community; affluence; opulence." The word wealth comes from the Middle English *welthe*, from well or weal, on the pattern of health (2). From this definition, we see that the first definition of wealth is prosperity and external happiness. Prosperity is primarily defined as (2): "PROSPER"ITY, n. [L. *prosperitas*.] Advance or gain in anything good or desirable..." Webster alludes that good external happiness is an outward display that reflects an inward happiness that comes from "God".

We know this because Noah Webster often listed Bible verses that use the referenced word. In the case of prosperity, he listed "The prosperity of fools shall destroy them. Proverbs 1:32." By this reference to fools, we see that prosperity can come from self or it can come from God to those the Bible describes as wise.

These definitions demonstrate that *wealth is an advance or gain in anything good or desirable toward the health and benefit of others.*" We also notice that the primary definition and use of the word wealth is *not tied to money or riches*. Historically however, one's health was a reflection of their ability to provide for their physical needs, but the origin of the word had nothing to do with being rich. Wealth, from the economic point of view, is determined by taking the total market value of all physical and intangible assets owned, then subtracting all debts. Essentially, wealth is the accumulation of resources. Specific people, organizations and nations are said to be wealthy when they are able to accumulate many valuable resources or goods. *Total of all assets of an economic unit that generate current income or have the potential to generate future income. It includes natural resources and human capital but generally excludes money and securities because they represent only claims to wealth. Two common types of economic wealth are (1) Monetary wealth: anything that can be bought and sold, for which there is market and hence a price.*[i]

Classical economists like Adam smith and his distinguished followers J.S. Mill, F.A. Walker, David Ricardo, etc. define economics as *"a science of wealth"*. Adam Smith is the leader of classical school of economic thought. There were many economists before the emergence of classical school of economic thought. However, the first definition was given by Adam smith. He categorized economics as a *separate science* which was linked with other subjects. For this great contribution of Smith in economic science, he is respected with the honor of *father of economics.* After the publication of Adam Smith's book (*An enquiry into nature and cause of wealth of nation*) in 1776 A.D[ii], economics got its independent identity. He defined economics *as the science which studies about the nature and causes of wealth of nation.*

According to him economics maintain the relationship between consumption and production of wealth. It is concerned with the knowledge of earning money. Every individual of the society has a desire to earn wealth. So, economics provides guidelines to the individual in earning more wealth.

The main points or ideas in the definition of Adam Smith are:
- *Study of wealth of nation:* Economics is the study of wealth of nation. It deals with consumption, production, exchange and distribution of wealth.
- *Study of economic activities:* Economics is only concerned with the activities of economic man, who is involved in earning more wealth. But it is not a study of non-eco-

nomic man, who is not involved in earning wealth.

- *Main goal is to earn wealth:* The main goal of human beings is to earn wealth because wealth is only the means for satisfying human wants.
- *First place to wealth*: Adam smith gave the first place to wealth and secondary place for man in the study of economics. In other words, the subject matter of economics is wealth. He advocated that man is made for wealth.
- *Only material goods constitute wealth:* The definition has given emphasize only material goods constitute wealth in society and there is no concern of economics with non-material goods or like free goods: —air, water, sunlight, water, etc. which do not play any role in creation of wealth in society.
- *Employed labor is the source of wealth:* The source of wealth of nation is employed labor whose productivity would be increased through the division of labor in production and distribution of goods and services.

Misconceptions about Wealth

Adam smith's definition of economics as a science of wealth has been criticized bitterly because it assumed wealth as *an end of human activities*. If it is accepted in life, there will be no place for love, sympathy, and patriotism and it had made the man selfish. Economists like Ruskin, Carlyle, Maris and Marshall, have criticized Adam Smith's definition as a *science of bread and butter*, a *science of getting rich*, a *dismal science*, a science of devil, etc. The major weakness or criticism points of this definition are as follows:

- *Narrow meaning of wealth:* Adam Smith considered that economics is the science of wealth and wealth includes only material goods. This is the narrow sense of defining wealth. In practice, wealth includes both material and non- material goods. The human wants can be fulfilled by using non material goods of services also.

- *Too much importance to wealth:* Adam Smith gave more importance to wealth than man. He had given first place for wealth and secondary place for human beings. But according to Marshall, *wealth is only a means of satisfying human needs.* Thus, economics must emphasize the study of man much more than the study of wealth.

- *No meaning of human welfare:* This definition gave no importance to the welfare of society. According to Marshall, the main aim of economics is to increase the welfare of human beings not to obtain wealth only.

- *Wrong assumption of economic man:* According to Adam Smith, Economic man is one who is involved in earning wealth and this economic man is only the subject matter of economics. But no man can be limited only with earning wealth. Because man is equally influenced by moral and spiritual thoughts like love, self-esteem, sympathy, friendship, etc.

- *Labor is not only the source of wealth:* According to Adam smith, main source of wealth is employed labor. In real, labor alone cannot produce anything. In production process, there are other factors of production like land, capital, and organization including labor.

What Does it Mean to be Rich?

Being rich is commonly described as possessing a large amount of money or assets. It originated from the (4) "Old English *rīce* 'powerful, wealthy,' of Germanic origin, related to Dutch *rijk* and German *reich*; ultimately from Celtic; reinforced in Middle English by Old French *riche* 'rich, powerful.'" The origination of this word ties together being rich with being powerful. Often richness is synonymously being used for wealth; however, richness has a very narrow connotation only referring to material possessions, money or assets and if not well balanced may leave the possessor unfulfilled, unsatisfied and unhappy. A balanced approach to the definition and understanding of wealth is needed to provide light in a broader sense.

Balanced Approach to Wealth

Wealth has to be approached in a multifaceted fashion in different aspects of life and not only limited to material possessions. It has to be looked from different perspectives such as economically, socially, physically, emotionally and spiritually in a holistic approach. Once we look at it in a more broader and inclusive sense it will help us to know exactly what to pursue, how to pursue and when have we acquired true wealth because we know exactly what it is. True wealth needs a healthy mind and spirit to fully manifest. A mind that is fed and challenged is a mind well used, it should be a personal goal to learn something new each day, even if that nugget of knowledge is banal in nature. True wealth is a wobbly three-legged stool in constant need of being balanced and that balance will be one's work. Once redefined wealth, one found greater happiness and sense of fulfillment in life.

> "—Wealth is achieving a state of unadulterated happiness with your life. It is when to some extent, you've known who you truly are, and you've achieved a balance in all the centers of your life i.e., economically, socially, physically, emotionally and spiritually."

Why is it important?

Economical: This is the case; to balance your life's centers it requires spending money most of the times. For instance, if your life's mission is to see the world, you will obviously need money to buy the tickets. If you want to get in shape, to make it easier, you will need to be eating some certain diets, and probably join a gym and all these will cost money. What I'm getting at here is that balancing all your centers will require spending money. So—*money is like a tool that we use, to achieve a wealthy lifestyle.* One thing about money to get into perspective is to figure out how much of it you will need in order to live a wealthy life. So, how much money is enough? What is your number? Everybody has one—if you don't have one already, it's time to get it. How much money will do it for you? There is a very good exercise about figuring out your number which I think everybody that wants a wealthy lifestyle should take part in. You do this task by making a list of all the aspects of your life that will require money. Also, it is imperative to think about the level of doing things in that aspect of your life that would make you really fulfilled and satisfied. For instance, under the traveling section, if you will feel happy taking two vacations yearly, to exotic locations, search for the cost of taking those vacations with all other expenses and put that number down. Remember, only you know what will make you happy and fulfilled —so, let your imagination soar!

While you are making the list, I don't want you to worry about "how" you are going to get this money. Leave that for later. For now, I want you to go nuts and make the assumption that getting the money is not an issue. Also, don't make the mistake of thinking that what you've written down cannot be amended at any point, because as time passes by, goals and dreams do change.

What Does Wealthy Mean to You?

The answer you came here to seek has been lying in you all along. You are the one that can answer that question. Nobody else has the ability to do it for you. So, I ask you again; with what you've read so far, what will wealth mean to you? Is it financial freedom, is it the love and respect of your family, whatever it is, my advice is that you should start working on it as soon as possible.

Chances are that if you don't work on it, you will always be sad and will always feel that your life is incomplete. And believe me when I tell you that all the tools you need to achieve this wealthy lifestyle you crave, have already been provided and programmed in you.

Physical: This is everything that relates to your body, this is the physical part of you. When you want to think about being wealthy, in the physical aspect, you mostly think about your health, how you feel, and the state of your body. Mostly, when this center of you is balanced, you are in good health and you are in good physiological state and can function optimally. It is hard to live a wealthy lifestyle when your body is suffering. Most people don't pay attention to their body until it is too late; when some form of disease has been developed, and life expectancy has been cut short.

Socially: This center has to do with your relationships and interactions with the other people in your lives. This might comprise of your family, your friends, your wife, your husband, your co-workers, your online friends, your customers, and so on. The relationships you hold in life can even be the stranger that you see walking down the street, whom you just wave casually to. How is your interaction with these people? Do you feel lifted and happy when you are with these people? When this center of your life is balanced, you have a profound relationship with those people in your lives. You often impact their lives positively and they also do the same in return. Most of the time, you are grateful for the people in your lives when you have a balanced social aspect

Emotionally: Have you ever heard the word "Emotional Intelligence"? Well, that is a new aspect of human psychology that is currently trending. People are now waking up to the need to get more emotionally smart. *—An emotionally intelligent person is a person that is in touch with his or her emotions.* Your emotions are basically how you feel about things. Those things might be what has happened, is happening, or will happen to you, or others. To cut the long story short, in order to be wealthy and have a balanced emotional life, we have to strive to be in control and master our emotions most of the time and enjoy the positive aspect of what they bring or avoid the negative results that might be produced by letting negative emotions take control. If something bad happens to someone that is balanced emotionally, he or she can feel sad about it for some time, but he or she is equipped with the ability to tune back to his or her happy and feel-good frequency, fairly quickly.

Spiritually: This is your connection to your inner self. Some people seek balance in this center through religion. While some people seek it from other places like their vocation, nature, science, wonders in the capability of the human race, and so on. The knowledge of the *"inner self"* is something that is often used as an anchor for the person that is able to achieve balance in this area. The deeper this anchor is; the more steadfast and ready the person is, to face the challenges of the current world and confidence for the one to come.

Balanced emotional and spiritual aspect result from carefully designed and crafted *"life mis-*

sion". This is what makes life worthwhile, and worth living in the first place.

So, what is a life's mission? I will employ the definition given by Charles Faulkner and Steve Andreas in their remarkable book; *NLP; The New Technology of Achievement;" A mission is a sense of purpose that lures you into your future. It unifies your beliefs, actions, and your sense of who you are. It's a fabric woven of the various threads of your interests, desires, and goals. Sometimes it's big, comprehensive, and even grandiose. Most of all, a mission is fun. When you are living your mission, you tend to behave like Steven Spielberg, who says, "I wake up so excited, I can't eat breakfast."iii*

Do you have that in your life? Do you have a purpose that gets your juices flowing? A mission is something that when you think about doing, you automatically start feeling good inside out. In my experience, a life's mission varies from person to person. Sometimes, it has nothing to do with money. For some people, it is a sense of higher calling that involves helping a lot of people in the process. For some people, it is all about finding peace, serenity, and connecting with the higher being or God. Some people have it as a mission to build a happy family with their wife and children. For some, it is about becoming the richest man in the world, while for some; it is being financially free and not having to answer to anybody for the rest of their lives. Whatever the mission might be, the common denominator among different life's mission is that; it is often bigger than the person with the mission, it matters a lot to the person, and it makes the person feel good. So, up until now, if you don't have a life's mission, it is time to start thinking about those things you are excited about, and start formulating your life's mission from those. Because, when you start living your mission (even if you haven't achieved the goals attached to the mission), you will be happier, and more emotionally and spiritually balanced.

The mission will serve as an anchor, or reference point of happiness, that you can refer to, anytime something screwball happens to you.

—Get a goal, to achieve your life's mission

How do we know when we have it?

The best way to recognize that we are wealthy is to look at the definition and observe the cardinal signs of wealth. It is possible to be wealthy and not be aware of that; because we have wrongly set our goals and priorities to life pursuit. As human beings, the quest to seeking wealth is an ongoing project and a life time endeavor; it should not be taken as a destination but rather a journey, not an event but a process. Striving for excellence and higher levels of satisfaction should be our mantra and motto, and keeping ourselves challenged to do better make life even more fulfilling and satisfying. It is not uncommon that we become excellent in one or two aspects and find ourselves wanting in other aspects of life.

Simple questions to ask ourselves include:-
1 *Economically, do I have enough money to achieve a wealthy lifestyle of my choice?*
2 *Physically, am I in a good physiological state to optimally live a wealthy and functional lifestyle?*

3 *Socially, do I have health interactions with the people I live with and surround me in my life?*

4 *Emotionally, am I emotionally intelligent enough to be in touch with my emotions, both positive and negative?*

5 *Spiritually, am I connected to my inner self and at peace with God?*

As you can see we are all in the journey to perfect ourselves and grow daily as we work on ourselves to become better on every aspect of life.

> *"You can only become truly accomplished at something you love. Don't make money your goal. Instead, pursue the things you love doing, and then do them so well that people can't take their eyes off you."*
>
> —*Maya Angelou*

[i] Business Dictionary
http://www.businessdictionary.com/definition/wealth.html
[ii] Adam Smith's —An enquiry into nature and cause of wealth of nation 1776 AD
[iii] NLP: The New Technology of Achievement, Steve Andreas and Charles Faulkner, 1996

two

Principles of Wealth Generation

"If you are going to achieve excellence in big things, you develop the habit in little matters. Excellence is not an exception, it is a prevailing attitude."

— *Colin Powell*

My mom told me a story as a little boy before going to bed one night; it was about a proud lion and a little mouse in the jungle of Africa. That story got stuck in my mind since then and I can't help but tell it to the world as it applies everyday in our normal lives. Once upon a time there was a mouse that went out and about in the jungle seeking for food and unfortunately got his tail stuck in a piece of old rugged oak tree fallen and half rotten. As he was there struggling for many hours to free himself the proud lion happened to pass by that way. The mouse howled for help from the lion. The lion came close to where the mouse was stuck, and the mouse pleaded for help with the promise that he will reciprocate the kindness provided there is an opportunity. The proud and strong lion stepped on the oak log, and the mouse's tail was freed. The mouse was very thankful and promised the lion that he too will freely help one day. But the lion looked down on the offer and said to him, don't worry pal, I've just helped you, no returns needed. The proud lion was thinking to himself —how could a small and little mouse like him help me anyhow? Days and months went by and one night, there was a great cry in the jungle and all animals were in awe of what was really happening in the deep silent night of the jungle as the lion's roars of crying could be heard miles away with a pleading for help. The mouse too heard the cry and went out to see what was happening —only to find his strong and powerful lion trapped; defenseless, destitute and helpless in the hunters' trap net. All other animals were astonished, standing by just staring, looking and doing nothing. The mouse stepped over and forward and told the lion not to worry he has a solution for his problem and in few minutes before the hunters came back he will be free. The lion was so surprised and couldn't believe what he was hearing; he just said to him, "I will appreciate your help." Well, the mouse went away and called all his friends and relatives, the vast army of mice showed up within few minutes and started chewing the ropes of the hunter's trap net and broke them in small pieces. Effortlessly they bit apart the entire net until it was all broken and the lion was cut loose! The mouse approached the lion with a wide smile and said to him, "I normally keep my promises." The moral of the story is simple, —*we all need each other, you can't be too small to provide help nor too big not to need help*. In every aspect of our lives that is socially, economically, financially, physically, emotionally and spiritually those surrounding us matter.

Normally people like to make friendship with wealthy people. You should note that there are two types of friendship. The first type of friendship is mutual relationship; this is where friends benefit from one another. The second type of friendship is the 'give me relationship'. In social life, some people seek friendship with you because they want to gain from you. They always want something from you and they come to you in form of friendship. When they are in need they will come to you in the name of friendship and say to you, "You are my friend please help me."But if you ask them at times to reciprocate the help that becomes the end of that friendship because now it's going to cost them something.

Success Principles

We all have access to the same success principles and wisdom of successful people. We are all born with the same blank canvas; we all have opportunity to become successful. Some of the greatest achievers in the world today came from very humble or even disastrous upbringings. Oprah Winfrey had extreme trauma in her early years. Sam Walton grew up in a poor farming family during the depression. Likewise, there are countless others who became titans in their industries despite having a disadvantaged childhood. What differentiates the ultra-successful from the mediocre then? Quite possibly, the disadvantage in their early years framed their thoughts and provided motivation as they grew. The reality is that there are certain success principles they —and others who achieve mega-success —follow and habits that they integrate that pave the way for success. Here is a look at some of the success principles that successful people share:

Principle1: Big, Small and Fast
Principle2: Do It Right
Principle3: Own Property
Principle4: Passive Incomes

Principle #1: Think Big, Start Small -Act Fast

All great businesses start small as much as many great people, leaders and super-achievers start with brand idea or a dream. These ideas are always in alignment with their great purpose and life mission. Almost every time, these ideas, dreams or visions are too big and they even fear to share with other people because they will be thought that they are going crazy. The irony is invariably all the times they have no clue of even how to implement it. First few weeks, months or years the dream becomes like a torturing chamber, the dreamer sees the glimpse of the future and what ought to happen but cannot comprehend how to get that future into today's reality. In other words, the practical ways of implementing that big idea has always been a major challenge to many of us. Too many dreams got aborted and abandoned at this stage because the dreamer gets overwhelmed by his or her own vision or dream and does not have a handle on how to make it happen. We call this *dreamers paralysis*, whereby the dreamer ends talking about the dream over and over for long period of time without any visible steps towards accomplishing it. My wife Dorothy calls them *"dreamers"* with a *"syndrome"*, and definitely they need some dose of encouragement, inspiration and technical how in order to get started. To start and dive straight into making the dream a reality is very difficult. The mantra *"Think Big, Start Small and Act Fast"* becomes the golden rule in the philosophy of dealing with *dreamer's paralysis.*

When it comes to accomplishing personal goals, everyone has his or her own style. Some people like to go ahead and broadcast their plans and ideas to the world what they're determined to achieve; others quietly work in their closets and never show anybody of what they are working on. As noted by Bahram Akradi[i] in his article, he says that some people are *"perfect preparers"* who spend months carefully laying the groundwork for future progress; others dive right in with a "damn the torpedoes" attitude they will figure out then whatever obstacles they might encounter. No one approach is better of the other because they depend much on the temperament, personality and commitment of the individual doing the committing and the nature of the goal.

Think Big

This philosophy propels the dreamer to develop an ambitious and expansive enough vision to get excited about what he or she is planning to achieve. Dull and mundane goals, or here we can call them *"chicken vision"*; tend to make for dull, unexcited and uninspired efforts. Going for the gold rather than silver pumps adrenaline in our system that gives us a reason to wake up in the morning and persist during the rainy days. The bigger your goal, the more you can motivate yourself to achieve it —someone said, *if you aim for a gold medal you might just get a silver; aim for a bronze and you'll be lucky to finish.* Small dreams can easily be accomplished and results in boredom, unexcited life and indulging into self-destructing behaviors due to lack of life challenging goals. Big dreams and mega goals have a tendency of attracting resources and people who are great thinkers and great minds around them as they realize this is a cause worth supporting.

> *"Results from a review of laboratory and field studies on the effects of goal setting on performance show that in 90% of the studies, specific and challenging goals led to higher performance than easy goals, "do your best" goals, or no goals. Goals affect performance by directing attention, mobilizing effort, increasing persistence, and motivating strategy development."[i]*

How can we break through the limitations we've set for ourselves? That's what Michael Port, author of The Think Big Manifesto, wants to know. "Sometimes we assign the role of 'Big Thinker' to some people, but we don't necessarily see ourselves in that role[ii]," he says. Often, that's because of "voices of judgment" —either negative peers or colleagues telling you why something will never work, or (even more damaging) your own internalized voice, telling you the same thing. But in order to truly thrive, he says, we have to let go of our self-imposed limitations —I can't talk to that person; she'll never hire me; that idea is too risky —and give things a try. Mark Batterson in his book "Chase The Lion: If the Dream Doesn't Scare You, It's Too Small[iv]" argues that this is a wake-up call to stop living as if the purpose was to simply arrive safely at death. Our dreams should scare us. They should be so big that without God they are impossible to achieve, we should quit running away from what we're afraid of but run towards it.

> "I dare you to think bigger, to act bigger, and to be bigger, and I promise you a richer and more exciting life if you do."
> —William Danforth

Start Small

Big things take time and require plans. But as the Great Prussian military strategist, von Moltke observed that the tactical result of an engagement forms the base for new strategic decisions because victory or defeat in a battle changes the situation to such a degree that no human acumen is able to see beyond the first battle. In other words, plans never survive contact with reality, so you need to *chunk the big thing into smaller things; while reminding yourself that these tedious smaller things are the path to the big thing, like pieces of the puzzle that has a bigger picture.*

The Chinese philosopher Lao Tzu had this figured out as well as he said, *"A journey of a thousand miles begins with a single step"* which I've interpreted to mean that it is the nature of the world that anything you seek to achieve needs to start with a single positive action in the correct direction of travel. That is why it is important to know first where you are going; even though directions may change many times but the destination remains!

Any dream or idea can be large and complex; but unfortunately, complexity is hard to manage and is daunting. It is hard to keep in your head not even starting to implement and becomes the reason for dreamer's paralysis. In fact the system's theorist, whose entire discipline was to understand the holistic workings of large and complex systems, decries the nature of complexity. Gall's Law is a rule of thumb for systems design from Gall's book[v]"Systemantics: How Systems Really Work and How They Fail". It states:

> *A complex system that works is invariably found to have evolved from a simple system that worked. A complex system designed from scratch never works and cannot be patched up to make it work. You have to start over with a working simple system.*
>
> —John Gall

Act Fast

The "*act fast attitude*" gets us focused on making continual progress and keeps our energy and enthusiasm high. It prevents us from getting so bogged down in the daily to-dos that we lose sight of the big picture that got us excited in the first place. "*Act fast*" also keeps us honest about the kinds of mini-goals we'll need to accomplish in order to make meaningful headway. Most major goals are marathons, not sprints, so it's important to pace ourselves. But part of pacing is setting challenging (not impossible) interim goals — benchmarks that give us constant feedback about the progress we're making and that help us recognize where adjustments to our plan might be necessary. Because rapidly correcting errors is an essential part of this whole approach. On the other hand, procrastination is a trap that many of us fall into. In fact, according to researcher and speaker Piers Steel[vi], 95 percent of us procrastinate to some degree. While it may be comforting to know that you're not alone, it can be sobering to realize just how much it can hold you back. Procrastination is often confused with laziness, but they are very different. Steel continues to say that *procrastination is an active process – you choose to do something else instead of the task that you know you should be doing.* In contrast, *laziness suggests apathy, inactivity and an unwillingness to act.* Procrastination usually involves ignoring an unpleasant, but likely more important task, in favor of one that is more enjoyable or easier. But giving in to this impulse can have serious consequences. For example, even minor episodes of procrastination can make us feel guilty or ashamed. It can lead to reduced productivity and cause us to miss out on achieving our goals. If we procrastinate over a long period of time, we can become demotivated and disillusioned with our work, which can lead to depression and even abandoning the entire dream or project, in extreme cases.

Mount Eagle College and University

The establishment of the Mount Eagle University came to us through lots of pain as the idea was conceived and brooded for more than 7 years. All the seven years my wife and I agonized with the conception that we could not deliver, as the popular saying *"do not tell us the pain; show us the baby!"* Until when the concept of chunking the dream and idea into small sizeable portion became obvious to us, then we took a bold but a baby step to start an establishment of a small institute initially. The humble beginnings soon gave us confidence and experience to go back and apply for an upgrade of an institute to become a college after 2 years then filed an application to became a full fledge university of which the approval was granted after 5 years. The great wisdom comes from an African (Swahili) proverb that says

"He who decides to take a cold shower never looks back."

—*Swahili Proverb*

The old and wise Zechariah in the ancient Scriptures reminds us by a rhetoric question that demands consideration. He asks —"Who despises the days of small beginnings?"Many successful endeavors and people have humble beginnings that they cherish and use as reference point to keep them humble and checked with their attained success. It is easy to forget where we came from and the struggles we went through before we got successful or achieved great goals. They will always be people below you that you need to inspire, motivate and encourage and nothing does best like your personal story of the struggles you had when you started.

Learn to protect your dream and ideas from *dream killers.* Don't rush to share your vision and dream with people who have no clue on how to take you to the next level. I'm personally guilty of this mistake by over-sharing my dreams with random people who end up discouraging, misleading or completely suffocating my visions to death. Often times, a big dream is like an eagle's egg that needs to be carefully protected in the nest, brooded and incubated for some weeks, months or even years before it hatches, and the young one has to learn how to survive and fly. Incubation for the American golden eagles is between 40-45 days. It can take a day for the hatchling to completely break free of the egg after pipping (cracking the egg). Golden eagles fledge in 7-11 weeks and prior to their first flight; nestlings will flap their wings in the nest or while jumping to an adjacent branch in behavior known as branching. Likewise to your idea, it needs *incubation period* where all the facts about your dream are collected and carefully analyzed and assessed. Even though the chicks have hatched; they are still dependent and cannot do much on their own and cannot fly yet. Dreams need *nurturing period* where much is invested initially and very little may be realized immediately. It's given time to grow, penetrate the market and establishes its presence. Some ideas take a short period while others take longer depending on the nature of the idea itself. And the third is *flying period* where the dream has broken loose and it becomes the reality to the dreamer.

Principle #2: Detours and Long Cuts Work

"There is no shortcut to success, take a long way and surely you'll arrive!" —*"shortcuts are always wrong cuts"* that's what my dad used to tell me over and over as a teenage boy. So many people are in such a hurry to success that they eagerly take any shortcuts that come across their way. In reality, shortcuts usually lead to disappointments rather than quicker success. The key to any long-term success is to take the necessary steps to steadily progress rather than skip any of them.

Success *is a mindset* and not a point in time but an inbuilt combination of character, discipline, behaviors and set of principles that make who the person becomes. Everything we ever been told about success usually revolves around a single point in time. I've seen gullible people buy into the many 'get rich quick' or 'lose weight fast' schemes out there only to find out that none of them work except in relieving you of the money paid for such products or programs. A friend of mine even bought one of those home devices that electronically stimulate belly muscle contractions thinking that weight loss is possible while watching TV and eating popcorn. This friend, who did not want to put in the work of exercising in a gym, is still overweight today. When we set a record, crash through the ribbon at the finish line, win the trophy, land the biggest customer in the history of our business. It's all about our "*spot emotional index*". Around key dates like graduation, end of the quarter, and bonus time, we feel successful if there is a physical memento to indicate that we were successful. Without the trophy it can be hard for us to gauge "*success*". That's why I go back to the idea that success is less a date on the calendar and more of a philosophy.

Success is a way of life
It's important that you adopt a successful mindset rather than aim for public indicators of success. Flashy public indicators of success attached to a pile of debt leave you unable to do the hard things that are required to realize your dreams. You can either look like "*the man*" or turn your dreams into reality, you can't really have both. Turning ideas into dreams and dreams into success is hard enough. It's a gut-wrenching, bloody nose battle that requires an absurdly special kind of toughness and steeliness in our nerves to take the pain for the long time. And when you are fighting for your dreams and the world is beating the life out of you; many times you might be tempted to try to take a shortcut. *Asking yourself: "Isn't there an easier way?"*And why not? Shortcuts look great on TV every time we watch them or on movies and success is granted immediately. Real life is little different, we live in time and era where success is fantasized as easy and many are delusional about a true and lasting success that comes from hard work, determination and

sacrifice. Remember, shortcuts will always hurt you, result in the loss of success and not help you in the long run. Here are a few key things to consider:

Taking shortcuts is admitting failure upfront.
It's pretty mentally damaging if you develop the habit of not trying to do things the right way. It's different from asking and seeking a better, convenient and more effective way of doing things. When your tendency to difficult life situation is a shortcut rather than focused intensity, you are admitting to yourself (and soon to others) that you are a failure. You may throw out your chest and claim to be on top of your game. But you know, deep down, that you have given up before you even started. I always challenge my students who would want to cheat on my exams to imagine the future and the implications of academic dishonesty as shortcut. How would it feel, few years from now; as a parent showing your academic accomplishment to your children in order to inspire them and soon you remember that few of those grades on your transcripts are actually not the true reflection of who you actually are because you cheated during exams. If you want to get your head back-on-straight look doubt in the eye and fight for your destiny. Get up two hours earlier, call three more people and ask for help and quit working on things that distract your focus and intend to be intense on what you do. You will be on the path to success and I promise the results will be obvious to you.

Taking shortcuts is the wrong reaction to fear.
When faced with the audacious challenge of being successful, we find ourselves at the crossroads of fight or flight. As soon as you decide you want to be something, and start to swim against the current, and set you mind to higher goals that are bigger than you, immediately you'll start to face resistance from the world. That resistance turns into oppression —people actively

fighting against your success. It's normal and natural to be afraid since those are inbuilt mechanisms for survival. But taking shortcuts is a flight reaction; not you fighting for your own success. Use fear to help drive effort and focus toward your mission. Use fear to build mental and emotional muscle around your purpose in life.

Taking shortcuts conflicts with the outrageous effort needed to be successful. The inherent idea that you can realize your wildest dreams without a passionate investment of mind, body, and soul is just nutty. You can't get more from your life by doing less. When you slow down and cheat yourself out of the self-investment necessary to build a brilliant destiny, you just won't ever find yourself where you want to be. To be successful, you have to work so hard till your eyes have blisters. Against all odds you have to keep trying —— when you're sick, when you're broke, when you have no fans, it is raw sweat equity. Taking shortcuts conflicts with everything that outrageous effort leads to—*it is to do nothing that means anything and still get everything.*

Taking shortcuts doesn't mean you end up where you wanted to be. Since there is rarely a certain, unchanging "end point" for success, you can't take a shortcut to a destination that doesn't exist. Have you ever thought you really wanted something, only to change your mind once you see what you got? You thought that you would be happy —and you weren't. Why? *Success is a process— a mindset.* And while success includes milestones, the emphasis is on the journey not on the original destiny. Most of us dream too small and we take our destiny and shrink it down into a small container that the critics can't get to. Life has an amazing way of helping you realize your dreams in ways far from what you could have ever imagined at the beginning of your dream. *In the world of dreams and vision, bigger is better, and there's no way to get there with a shortcut.*

So I encourage you to dream bigger than ever and don't steal your chance at an amazing destiny by taking a shortcut; it's not fair to you. Take the same steps as other successful people have done. Although it is wise to get proper coaching, instruction and mentoring for your goals, these are not considered shortcuts. They are just more efficient and effective ways to learn the skills required for success. However, time with a coach or instructor does not replace the steps one must take in order to be successful. You still have to do your part of the work whether it's working out at the gym, building wealth, starting a new relationship or practicing your ski turns on the bunny hill. The bottom line is that there are no true shortcuts to real success. Many of the goals we want to achieve have already been achieved by countless numbers of other people. Follow their examples and take the same type of steps they had to take in order to be successful. Each step is very much like a little success on its own and little successes do add up. Pay your dues to steadily develop towards success rather than take detours on shortcuts that can actually set you back.

Principle #3: Real Estate Investment

Real estate investing is the purchase, ownership, lease, or sale of land and any structures on it for the purpose of earning money. Real estate generally breaks down into three categories: residential, commercial, and industrial.

Residential real estate: Residential real estate consists of single family homes, multi-family homes, townhouses, condominiums, and multi-family homes that people use as a living space and not a working space. Homes that are larger than four units are considered commercial property. Some examples include free-standing homes, townhouses, and condominiums that occupants can own.

Commercial real estate: Commercial real estate is property that is used for the purpose of business. Commercial real estate is classified as office, retail, land or multi-family. Some examples of commercial real estate properties include business offices (office), restaurants (retail), farmland (land), and large apartment buildings (multi-family).

Industrial real estate: As the name suggests, these properties serve an industrial business purpose. Some examples include shipping or storage warehouses (godowns), factories, and power plants.

Each category of real estate and type of investment carries its own set of risks and rewards. Regardless of the type of real estate that you invest in, it is important to choose investments wisely by running opportunities through a rigorous underwriting process. No matter who performs the underwriting, due diligence plays a vital role in making a decision on an investment determining whether an investment opportunity is financially sound and whether it can meet your financial goals. Many investors like to use a projected rate of return as a key metric when analyzing real estate. However, more seasoned real estate investors will often turn to capitalization rate, or "cap rate," as a preferred way to assess an opportunity.

Ways to Invest in Real Estate

There are a multitude of ways to invest in real estate with any amount of money, time commitment, and investment horizon. Real estate investment options break down into two major categories: *active* and *passive* investments. Here are seven fundamental ways to invest in real estate with options ranging from intense, high-effort to hands-off low-effort.

Active Real Estate Investing (Doing it Yourself):
Active real estate investing requires a great deal of personal real estate knowledge and hands-on management or delegation of responsibilities. Active investors can work as real estate investors part-time or full-time, depending on the nature and number of their investment properties. They usually invest in properties with only one or a few owners, so they bear quite a bit of responsibility in ensuring the success of a property. Because of this, active real estate investors need real estate and financial acumen and negotiation skills to improve their cap rate and overall return on investment.

House-Flipping: House-flipping is a type of active-real estate investing. It is the most active, hands-on way to invest in real estate. In a house flip, an investor purchases a home, makes changes and renovations to improve its value on the market, and then sells it a higher price. House-flipping is generally short-term, because the longer the investor owns the home without leasing it to tenants, the more their expenses add up. This eats away at returns when they sell it. Investors can repair or renovate the home to increase its sale price or sell when its value in the housing market increases. Another property-flipping option is *wholesaling.* Wholesaling is when an investor signs a contract to buy a property that they believe is underpriced and then sells it quickly to another investor at a higher price for a profit. .

Rental Properties: Rental properties also require hands-on management, but unlike house flips, they have a long-term investment horizon. Any type of property (residential, commercial, or industrial) can be a rental property. Property owners earn regular cash flow usually on a monthly, quarterly, biannually or annual basis in the form of rental payment from tenants. This can provide a steady, reliable income stream for investors, but it also requires a lot of work or delegation of responsibilities to ensure that operations are running smoothly.

Airbnb: Airbnb[vii] is a tech company that allows residents to rent out their homes on a nightly basis, usually as an alternative to a hotel. Airbnb rentals are similar to rental properties, but they are confined to residential properties and usually only available for short-term periods. Unlike traditional rentals, Airbnb lets you rent out a portion of your home, or your entire home. Property owners earn money by renting their property by the night, which can provide regular or irregular cash flow, depending on the demand of the property within its specific market. Property owners are responsible for furnishing and maintaining the home for renters. Airbnb rentals require much less expertise and supervision than traditional rentals for several reasons. Airbnb itself facilitates the booking of the rental property and creates the contract agreement between the property owner and renter.

Because Airbnb manages several components of the rental process, Airbnb rental properties can be a part-time job or side hustle. While Airbnb rentals can be a lucrative solution to the spare bedroom in your home, before listing, make sure that short-term rentals are allowed in your area. Homeowner associations have the power to ban short-term rentals, and in some cities, such as New York, there are existing bans against types of short-term rentals. And, make sure that you're prepared to handle any possible headaches that may come up under Airbnb's hosting policies.

Real estate has a track record of strong performance. Real estate investing offers the potential to earn significant returns and add meaningful diversification to your portfolio as an investor at all levels. When managed wisely it can become a valuable source of cash flow in your investment portfolio. As with any investment, real estate investments require you to understand and weigh the risks and potential rewards before beginning.

Like in any investment, learn from successful people who have demonstrated results in real estate. Be careful from where you learn, do not take advise from people who are mediocre or have failed in the area. If you're an engineer don't ask the medical doctor to train you in engineering! You will end up been discouraged and demotivated to pursue your dream.

Wise people learn from their own mistakes. Smart people learn from other people's mistakes, and they avoid doing those mistakes. But great people learn from successful people.

Great people don't have time to learn from their own mistakes because it is costly and leaves a lot of scars behind. They have learned the art of imitating the successful people, they run fast to catch up with them. Some cultures hate and disown successful people, they don't want tolearn from them but instead they excommunicate them, marginalize and if possible incriminate them for crimes they never committed because of jealousy. In contrast, other cultures especially in the western world, people idolize achievers and celebrities. They would like to be close to successful people and want to learn the secret of their success. Tom Corley in his book "Rich Kids: How to Raise Kids to be Happy and Successful in Life" says that poor people have poor habits and do hate rich and successful people[viii].

Linda McKissack and her husband were

$600,000 in debt when they made a real estate decision that turned their lives around. Today, the McKissack Realty Group sells over $60 million and over 300 properties each year. McKissack says their biggest success is not their property sales; it's how they learned to generate over $250,000 a year in passive income and achieve financial freedom through real estate.

Speaking of real estate, although it might not work out for you and it's not right for everyone, it has certainly worked out for others. Interview from colleagues and friends on just how quickly real estate investing can help individuals build wealth; here's what some have to say:

> *Real estate investing may not make you wealthy overnight, but it can add zeros to your net worth in a shorter timeframe than many other traditional investments. For example, purchasing a fixer-upper house, rehabbing the property, and selling it for more can net you a significant windfall if you do it correctly. Just be sure to buy low, rehab smart, and sell fast. House flipping, as this process is called, is largely a math game, and significant profits can be made by those willing to take on the challenge.*
> —Brandon Turner

Principle #4: Multiple Streams

Multiple streams of passive income is the most efficient way to build wealth–but not the only one. Researchers have even pinpointed a statistic: millionaires, on average, have not just one, but seven streams of income. Few questions might pop in your mind; first, is seven the magical number of income streams that turns you into a millionaire, or is it that the millionaires know how important multiple streams of income are, and so begins to "collect" them? Second, are those seven types of streams, or could those seven streams be in the same category (for example, real estate)?Finally, do highly-paid professionals really need this many streams of income or should they just keep working hard in their given profession? Let's try to answer these questions systematically here:

Do the Income Streams Make the Millionaire, or Is It the Other Way Around?

Well, the number seven may not be magical, but it does seem these concepts are two sides of the same coin. Yes, the streams may eventually make the millionaire, but it's also true that the millionaire understands the importance of multiple income streams–without them; after all, he or she may never have broken the million-dollar mark. So, he or she continues to increase their streams of income.

Are These Seven Individual Categories of Streams, or Are They All from the Same Category?

As with all investments, I believe that it makes the most sense to diversify your streams of income. That is, up to a point. If you're finding a category that works for you, then go for it. Still, don't put all of your eggs in one basket, diversification is the key here. I'm talking about the whole picture here – not only the way you gain income and increase net worth, but also what you do with it. Smart people have learned that the best way to build wealth is to turn your active income into multiple passive income machines.

Should You Focus on Building More Streams of Income, or Is Your Profession the Top Priority?

Highly-paid professionals (like doctors, engineers, accountants, lawyers, consultants etc.) should definitely be looking into multiple streams of income. In fact, more than anyone, we are in the best position to accelerate our growth towards financial freedom. We're able to earn the necessary capital and immediately throw that money into creating additional streams. We just have to be strategic about it. Keep your expenses in check, and be disciplined about moving your earned income from your day jobs and straight into the money-making machines. There is a balance to be made here; you just have to figure out exactly where it is for you.

Different Streams of Income

If you've made it this far, hopefully we're (at least somewhat) on the same page. And if so, you may be wondering about what these seven streams might actually consist of. Well, while there's no perfect blueprint for what these income streams should be, here are some of the most common types of streams:-

- *Earned Income*—This is your day job and most people's primary source of income. this one's easy to understand and most people's primary source of income. You trade your time for money.

- *Business Income*—You own a business. You either make and sell something, or you provide a service.

- *Interest Income* —This is income you make from lending your money out. This might mean a CD, P2P lending, real estate crowdfunding, funding fix-and-flip debt deals, or simply money in a savings account.

- *Dividend Income*—This is money that's distributed as a result of owning shares of a company.

- *Rental Income* —You own something and you rent it out. Probably the most common is owning a rental property, such as a multifamily apartment building (renting apartments in exchange for monthly payments).

- *Capital Gains* —This is money earned when you sell an investment, like stocks.

- *Royalties and Licensing*—You create a product, idea, or process, and you let someone use it. They pay you a small fee every time they do.

Venture into Entrepreneurship

I highly recommend you start building wealth by venturing into entrepreneurship if you haven't considered that. When I became an entrepreneur, my wealth-building journey really took off. Several years prior, I had read the book Rich Dad Poor Dad[ix]. In that book, author Robert Kiyosaki introduces the concept of the cash flow quadrant. He looks at four different entities: the employee, the self-employed, the business owner, and the investor. When I read that book I fell under the employee quadrant, but I knew that if I ever wanted to make serious money, I had to get into the right type of quadrant – either the business owner or the investor quadrant (the investor quadrant is actually the best).When I first started as a professor, I was still an employee. I didn't have the ability to make my own hours and to grow my business as much as I could, because I had a lot of restrictions. My first step was crossing over into being self-employed. Just by making that shift, I saw a 30% increase in income in my first year. Since then, I've become a business owner – and now I consider myself also to be an investor.

Guy Kiyosaki talks about quadrant of cash flow, which

has are four types of income streaming as explained below:-

E = Employee
People who works for others.

As an employee, you will earn monthly income, no matter the company you work for gained profit or not. But what if for any reasons you could not work anymore? As an employee, there's a Boss who take control of you. Otherwise, how much maximum income could you earn?

ACTIVE INCOME

B = Business Owner
You are the Boss.
You are manifesting people's time, mind, and energy to makes money for you.

PASSIVE INCOME

E B

S I

S = Self Employee
You are the Boss and employee as well.
Example: doctor, lawyer, and actor/actress

As a self-employed, you don't have Boss. no one give you order. You can work anytime you want. Your income depends on your working time The longer you work, the more you earn. But what if for some reasons they couldn't work anymore? Will you still get income?

I = Investor
Money works for you

If you had a lot of money, just have put on investment. Such as paper sheets, deposit account, and property.

E—Employee
S—Self employed
B—Business owner
I—Investors

E—Employee
Most individuals only live in this area. You work for a company and trade your time for money. If you want to earn more money, you must work more hours. Another option is work for another company that pays better. With this position in the quadrant there is no passive income. If you don't work, you don't make any money. You are employed by somebody else and unfortunately you don't make profit. You are trading your energy, creativity, intellect and time for a salary from your employer. That means you exchange your poten-

tial with salary and there is no leverage here. Employee falls on the active side of income stream quadrant and it's okay to start somewhere but this should not be the destination but a starting point.

S—Self employed

This is one step better than an employee, but in reality you still are trading time for money. You own your own business, but in reality the business owns you. The positive benefit is that you have more personal and financial freedom than an employee. Here someone is self-employed and makes profit. Time is everything for the self-employed individual. People in this category may include professionals such as doctors, accountants, engineers, lawyers, architects, consultants etc. They work very hard and it is very risky. People of this category take every precaution to see that they don't get a loss, fall sick or miss work. They literally don't have time for social gatherings. Self-employed category is still on the active side of income stream quadrant.

B—Business owner

A business implies you have a system in place. You have others working for you as employees. You aren't selling your time for money, but rather selling a product or service. In other words, you don't have to be working for the business to generate income. This is one of the passive income streams. You own the system and people work for you and you pay them salary. This is not one man's show. You need to employ other people. Here you are leading not like on self-employment where you are managing the business. Everything else is delegated except thinking. You redeem time and increase productivity as you get enough time to think. Business ownership category is on the passive side of income stream quadrant.

I—Investment

This is where you truly have passive income. Investments like stocks, bonds, and real estate generate an annual cash flow. These are the investments that will allow you to retire. It can also be things like trademarks, copyrights, and royalties. Things you build once and have a long (5-10 year plus) timespan in payouts. Here money is working for you and you are not working for it. What you get you invest it back in the system to generate more money. The business you are doing gives you investment opportunities.

In multiple passive incomes it is advised to have at least four sources of income to get started on your journey to generating wealth. When one source dries out at least you still have three other sources flowing. One stream of income is not enough and as stated earlier, there are seven different categories of passive income.

> *Self-employed people make up less than 20 percent of the workers in America but account for two-thirds of the millionaires.*
> *—Thomas J. Stanley*

[i]Think Big, Start Small, Move Fast By Bahram Akradi | October 2017 https://experiencelife.com/article/think-big-start-small-move-fast/

[ii]Locke et al, Goal setting and task performance: 1969–1980. Psychological Bulletin, Vol 90(1), Jul 1981, 125–152.

[iii]Michael Port (2009); The Think Big Manifesto: Think You Can't Change Your Life (and the World) Think Again. Publisher: Gildan Media;

[iv] Mark Batterson, (2016); Chase The Lion: If the Dream Does Scare You, It's Too Small. Publisher Doubleday Religious Publishing Group

[v] John Gall (1975); Systemantics: How Systems Really Work and How They Fail. p.71

[vi] Steel, P. (2007). The nature of procrastination. Psychological Bulletin, 133(1), 65-94.

[vii] Airbnb https://airbnb.com

[viii] Tom Corley (2014) Rich Kids: How to Raise Kids to be Happy and Successful in Life Two Harbors Press, MN

[ix]Robert Kiyosaki and Sharon Letcher (1997)Rich Dad Poor Dad.

three

Pitfalls of the Wealth Pursuit

"True wealth is not the matter of bank accounts and assets. It is in the value we live and share as well as people we keep in touch and care."
—Unknown

Greek mythology has a story of King Midas, being a king and knowing how powerful money is, asked that everything he touched be instantly turned to gold. Sounds like a quick way to become rich, doesn't it? The king's plan started out great! On his way home he touched trees and rocks and watched gleefully as they turned to gold. Once he arrived back at the palace, he asked his servants to make a huge feast to celebrate. Hungry from his journey, he picked up food to eat. But to his surprise and disappointment, the food turned to gold before he could eat it. The king knew he would not be able to survive. Things only got worse for Midas, however. When his daughter came to give him a hug, she turned to gold. If King Midas didn't do something, both he and his daughter would die.

King Midas realized the dark side of his wish as he held his daughter who had turned into gold. Midas realized that he had made a huge mistake and his greed had gotten him into a grave situation. He asked how to reverse the wish and was told that if he bathed in the river, he would return to normal. Midas quickly went to the river and watched as the water and sand turned to gold. Midas, realizing that more material possession and gold is not always a good thing, promised to give up his desire for riches. He went off and lived the rest of his life in the country, away from the splendor of the palace.

Moral of the story is we should always think very deeply before making choices. Each choice we make has its own consequences so we need to make wise choices. In our modern world because we are so eager to make money from our resources and everything around us, so many times we do not pay much attention to relationships, ethics, nature and beauty just as King Midas turned everything into gold because he was so greedy.

Many believe that our desire to accumulate wealth and the unintended consequences of these desires are modern day inventions. The mythical King story reveals that in ancient Greek culture, the wealthy were also preoccupied with becoming richer. The story shows what happens when people lose focus on what is truly important. This is a man who goes to great lengths to become the wealthiest person in the world. He wishes that whatever he touches shall turn to gold. His wish comes true. At first, he loves the fact that his clothes, bed, and even his rose garden become golden. But, when he can't eat his food or hug his daughter because they also turn to gold, he becomes extremely upset and wishes that he could take everything back. Isn't it most people's ambition to be economically and financially wealthy? Though not many people would admit to it, many people would stop at nothing to achieve such great goal. That is until their ambition backfires and they lose what is really important to them.

> *"Money doesn't change men, it merely unmasks them. If a man is naturally selfish or arrogant or greedy, the money brings that out, that's all."*
> — *Henry Ford*

Pursuit of economic wealth doesn't have to be a mutual exclusive endeavor; it can encompass other important aspects of life considered in their rightful perspective. One of the greatest ways not to fall in King Midas' pitfall is to create core values that will guide us in the pursuit of economic wealth.

Core Values as an Anchor

Creation of core values is the greatest antidote to help us remain in focus and not lose the bigger picture. They are the fundamental beliefs of a person or organization; guiding principles that dictate behavior and can help people understand the difference between right and wrong. It is understood that core values help companies to determine if they are on the right path and fulfilling their goals by creating an unwavering guide. The core values of an organization are those values we hold which form the foundation on which we perform work and conduct ourselves. We have an entire universe of values, but some of them are so primary, so important to us that throughout the changes in society, government, politics, and technology they are *still* the core values we will abide by. In an ever-changing world, core values are constant. They are *not descriptions of the work* we do or *the strategies we employ* to accomplish our mission. These values underlie our work, how we interact with each other, and which strategies we employ to fulfill our mission. They are the basic elements of how we go about our work. They are the practices we use (or should be using) every day in everything we do.

Organizations, companies or individuals without core values are exactly like a boat without an anchor; it can be easy tossed to and fro following any direction the wind blows.

The following are the benefits of having core values:

- Govern personal relationships

- Guide business processes

- Clarify who we are

- Articulate what we stand for

- Help explain why we do business the way we do

- Guide us on how to teach and train others

- Inform us on how to reward

- Guide us in making decisions both small and big

- Underpin the whole organization

- Require no external justification

Core Values Are Not:
- Operating practices

- Business strategies

- Cultural norms

- Competencies

- Changed in response to market/ administration changes

- Used individually

Personal core values are vitally important because they are part of us. They highlight what we stand for and they can represent our unique, individual essence. They guide our behavior, providing us with a personal code of conduct and when we honor our personal core values consistently, we experience fulfillment. When we don't, we are incongruent and are more likely to escape into bad habits and regress into childish behavior to uplift ourselves.

> *Your personal core values define who you are, the company's cover values ultimately defines the companies character and brand. For individuals, character is destiny, for organizations, culture is destiny.*
> —*Tony Hsieh*

Most of us don't know our values as we don't understand what's most important to us. Instead, we focus on what our society, culture and media values. Can you articulate your top 5 to 10 values that are most important to you? Without undergoing a discovery process, it's challenging to identify your personal core values. It's easy to speculate and idealize what you *should* value. But knowing and accepting what you value takes effort. While the following process is best done with a qualified coach, you can do it on your own if you apply self-honesty, patience, and determination.

The following are the simple steps as advocated by Scott Jeffrey[i], the leadership and business coach; towards discovery of the personal core values. Take out your journal, a notepad, or a note-taking app. Here are 7 steps to creating distinct and meaningful core values that will serve you in every area of your life.

Step One: Beginner's Mindset
It's too easy to presume that we know the answer at the start and to, therefore, never embark on a creative, personal discovery process. Adopt the mind of a beginner; someone with no preconceived notions of what is has more chances to assimilate more awareness and teachability.

Step Two: Create Your List
Normally to get to a list of about ten individual core values can become a daunting task. For those who have never done this before it's worth mentioning that you could scan online to get an idea of what are the core values that can be ap-

plied at the personal level. However, it is not recommended because values aren't selected; but discovered and revealed. At the end of this chapter, I put listed some of the individualized core values in category to help you with the process.

Step Three: Assign Richer Context
Highlighting values into memorable phrases or sentences helps you articulate the meaning behind each value. It gives you the opportunity to make the value more emotional and memorable.

Use inspiring words and vocabulary since our brains are quick to delete or ignore the mundane and commonplace. Be mindful of words that evoke and trigger emotional responses. They will be more meaningful and memorable. Make your value statements rich and meaningful to you so they inspire you to uphold them. You could use other words from the groupings of the category for example; let's say you've identified a core value of health to represent other values, like energy and vitality. Your values statement might be: *"Health: to live with full vitality and energy every day."*

Decision Making Process
Knowing your personal core values and their order of priority is helpful in making difficult decisions in life. Then, imagine your life several months or years from now having made that decision. For example, what will your new business or a family change your life? Step into this future picture as much as you can and make it come alive in your mind. Now, score your personal values while keeping the vision alive in your mind. Does deciding elevate your values score? Does it

cause friction with one of your higher values? This process will help bring a new level of clarity to your decision-making process

Bring Former Clients?

Few years back, our company was signing a new partnership agreement with a couple who terminated their contract with a different company and decided to join our firm. Part of the agreement for this couple was to engage in marketing activities to increase our client base locally and in the neighboring cities. The couple offered to bring more than 100 clients from their former partnership because of the loyalty they had developed to them. That was a big boost for our business which by the time it was struggling with a handful of clients. On the negotiating table; we said that we appreciated their offer of 100 clients; we really would love to have them on our portfolio but unfortunately, that is against our core values and the golden rules for this company. —*We would not do anything that we would not want others to do to us.* In amazement, the couple couldn't believe what they were hearing from us. We stood firm on that decision despite the fact that everybody in the industry does it but us; this is our highest ranking core value that cannot be compromised. In our marketing strategies, we do not harvest from other people's barns or fish from other's baskets. In other words, we made it clear that we do not solicit clients that already have serving agencies to change service providers to us; we normally approach new clients that are not committed and sell our services to them. Well, one person affirmed to us that we will be out of business by this time next year; on contrary our business grew 5 times the following year.

The Downfalls of Sacrificing for Wealth

People sacrifice time with kids or spouses because of business, work and vocational choices. As a founder and leader, your job is never done. It comes with the territory of starting a business or being the captain of your ship that you'll need to sacrifice a little blood, sweat, tears (money, time— the list could go on) to achieve success. But at a certain point, if all you're doing is making sacrifices, perhaps you're paying too high a cost for that success. Check out the list below. Do any of these signs sound familiar? Maybe it's time to rethink your priorities[ii]:

You sacrifice your family time for work.
I am guilty of this one myself. Using the excuse that I need to feed my family might seem acceptable at an early stage, but it's still an excuse. Take a serious look at your overall time investment. Don't count the hours you are in the office. Count the hours you answer emails on your phone, the time you drive to work, the time you spend thinking about work, and the time you have left for everything else. Many times we are not present mentally but working and bogged down with office work while we are physically at home. We become emotionless, absent and occupied with work while family gets the exhausted cramps of hours that remain on the table.

Nobody on their dying bed wished they had spent more time at the office or working but had time with the family and loved ones.

—Facts of Life

Your work and leisure time always intersect.
This one is hard for many people, mostly because the job can be fun at times. Playing around with a new app on the iPad doesn't seem like work. No matter which field you're in, it's best to figure out where the delineation lies between actual work and actual relaxation. Sometimes, you have to be intentional about this: take up tennis as a recreational sport because it has nothing to do with your cooking business. While work is changing and some entrepreneurs have to work extremely long hours to kick-start a company, having no margins means you are not working that smart anyway.

You can't take time off.
I've been reading the book "The Everything Store" about how Jeff Bezos became such a celebrity entrepreneur. In his early days, he had a camping bed with a little mattress (cot) in his office in case he needed to sleep at work. I too am the victim of that. If that's you, think long and hard about whether it makes sense. Maybe in an early-stage startup it seems reasonable. But the truth is that your inability to take time off from work is a sign that you have poor boundaries and I bet someone is paying for that extremism, listen to your spouse or children very carefully.

You're constantly living in stress and anxiety.
There is scientific proof that constant stress is chipping years off your life, and it's not worth the strain. By thinking about work from sun-up to sundown, you are fixating your brain on one thing. Extremism at work is a way to control the work, but it usually backfires. In most cases, business needs time to grow and evolve. If it's 9 p.m. at night and you are thinking about a sales meeting the next morning, then you don't have good margins. If raking in the cash means a shorter life, live on less.

Your gadgets are always on.
I seem to always have an iPhone at the ready, which is easy to justify. But letting the plastic gizmos die once in a while is a good thing. When your phone or tablet is not available to you, it forces you to look outside once in a while, to have a conversation with someone, to think about something besides work. In science jargon, this is called sensory dynamism. When you stare at the iPhone, you are only experiencing a few planes of reality. When you look outside, you are seeing millions and your brain needs a reprise from the gadgets, and overuse is not advised healthwise.

You have no friends.
If the only relationships you have are at work, you might have a problem. Workaholics have plenty of income and no social life. In some cases, that's okay for a while. But take a long look at whether you are actively developing friendships outside of work. True friends will tell you when you are working too much; business colleagues will just

encourage you to work more because they reap the rewards. You might end up with a big successful company, but life is about more than just financial success.

Unethical Dealings

Businesses engage is unethical or scrupulous practices to maximize profit or get rich quick schemes. *Ethics* can be defined as going beyond what is legal and doing what is right, even when no one is looking. Unethical behavior is an action that falls outside of what is considered morally right or proper for a person, a profession or an industry. Individuals can behave unethically, as can businesses, professionals and politicians. So when we talk about *unethical* behavior in business, we're talking about actions that don't conform to the acceptable standards of business operations, failing to do what is right in every situation. In some cases, it may be an individual within a business who is unethical in the course of his or her job and at other times, we're talking about corporate culture, where the whole business is corrupt from the top down, with disastrous results for society. It's important to realize that what is unethical may not always be illegal (though sometimes it is both). There are many instances where businesses may act within the law, but their actions hurt society and are generally considered to be unethical.

Unethical Behavior Among Individuals
- Lying to your spouse about how much money you spent.

- Lying to your parents about where you were for the evening.

- Stealing money from the petty cash drawer at work.

- Lying on your resume in order to get a job.

- Talking about a friend behind his back.

- Taking credit for work you did not do.

- Cheating on a school paper by copying it off the Internet.

- Cashier mistakenly returns more money and you decide to keep it.

- Taking $20.00 out of your friend's wallet when he is sleeping.

- Using your position of power at work to sexually harass someone.

- Selling a house and not disclosing known defects to the buyers.

- Selling a car and lying about the vehicle's accident history.

Unethical Behavior Among Businesses
- Dumping pollutants into the water supply rather than cleaning up the pollution properly.

- Releasing toxins into the air in levels

above what is permitted by the Environmental Protection Agency.

- Coercing an injured worker not to report a work injury to workers' compensation by threatening him with the loss of a job or benefits.

- Refusing to give an employee a final paycheck for hours worked after the employee leaves the company.

- Not paying an employee for all of the hours worked or delaying their payment for not justifiable reason.

- Incorrectly classifying an employee as an independent contractor and not as an employee in order to reduce payroll taxes and avoid purchasing unemployment and workers' compensation insurance.

- Engaging in price fixing to force smaller competitors out of business.

- Using bait and switch or false advertising tactics to lure customers in or convince them to buy a product.

- Rolling back the odometer on a vehicle that is for sale.

- Refusing to honor a warranty claim on a defective product.

Unethical Behavior by Professionals
- Doctors, dentists, and lawyers dating their clients, or professors dating their students.

- Not telling a patient his true diagnosis because the physician didn't know the details of the diagnosis.

- A dentist performs unnecessary procedures on a patient in order to receive the insurance payment.

- Using a patient as a teaching tool for students for long periods of time without the permission of the patient or patient's family.

- A lawyer will not return money or provide which was being held for a client.

- A lawyer represents parties on both sides of a legal transaction.

Unethical Behavior Among Politicians and the Government
- Using the Internal Revenue Service (IRS) to target groups that you do not like by auditing those groups or refusing to give them tax exempt status.

- Obtaining private tax information about your political opponents from the Internal

Revenue Service and using that information in a campaign.

- Knowingly telling lies about your own political position or about the political position of your opponent just to get elected.

- Accepting excess campaign contributions that violate campaign finance laws.

- Using money that was donated to your campaign for personal, non-approved expenses.

- Using your position of power to coerce lobbyists into buying expensive gifts for you and for your wife.

These are just some of the many different examples of unethical behavior that could occur.

Betrayal of Trust

People betray each other's trusts in partnerships or workplace in order to gain material possession and hurt many lives. Let us consider the human process of trust, we find that *trust is hard to gain and easy to lose.* It usually takes a while to build trust with employees, among team members or with customers. Unfortunately, it doesn't take much to lose that trust – often only one or two unfortunate incidents will reset attitudes. Worse still, once trust has been broken by a missed commitment or betrayal, it takes even longer to restore it to its previous level. One heuristic states that for every one failure, we have to demonstrate five positive behaviors to begin to recover trust. And recovering from a second failure is almost impossible. As they say, *"Fool me once, shame on you. Fool me twice, shame on me"*.

Why does this matter? Well, in any organization trust between colleagues is the foundation of business performance because it is directly related to empowerment. We will play our role on the team because we trust you will play yours. With trust, the speed of implementation goes up and the cost to get things done goes down. Decisions can be made more quickly. There is less likely to be duplicated effort and more likely to be innovation. This also applies to customer and partner relationships. With trust, negotiations are easier, decisions get made faster and both parties benefit from greater collaboration. Any good salesperson understands this and works hard to earn and preserve the trust of her or his clients. It's easier to keep an existing customer (or employee) than to find a new one – because the trust is already there.

It is always wise to think twice before taking actions that could damage relationships. As business people we are often forced to make the trade-off between short term gain and long term relationships. Do we give a margin-destroying customer discount to compensate for poor service or a delivery error? Do we forego employee salary increases in order to meet our earnings targets? Do we push some cost over to a partner or customer in order to reduce our own? Do we limit the number of participants in our program or event to control our costs? In all cases we're putting our self-interest ahead of our partner's. It won't be long before our partner gets the message and our relationship is impacted accordingly.

Any good relationship can absorb some selfishness, but the effect is cumulative and can reach a tipping point unexpectedly. Once you've fallen off that cliff, it's a long slow climb back up the mountain to regain your position of trust.

Neglect of Health

There must be a reason why lots of startup entrepreneurs who are hustling very often ignore their own health. I think there is a serious problem in time management and setting of priorities. Entrepreneurs especially who have started-up struggle hard to prioritize their time and health comes last in their to-do list. You will very often hear them complaining about lack of time, but personally I do not think time is an issue. Poor time management skill is what is driving these super humans crazy. We do become the boss in planning our day but that boss has no control over their own well-being. What is the point of being a boss of our own destiny when we are not taking good care of our body, which is supposed to enjoy the perk of all our hard work? The journey which is the whole essence of being an entrepreneur or business person is not being enjoyed fully. The freedom which we longed for as an entrepreneur, leader, business person or pioneer is now becoming the dangerous evil, this very freedom has started to act against us.

What is the solution?
We can't simply complain about lack of time and

move ahead, especially if you are founder of any organization, you are not alone, you are accountable for people who are putting their trust on you, and if you are not healthy enough how can you delegate the responsibilities in a healthy manner. Being an unhealthy founder can only lead to an unhealthy organization. Your behavior, your managerial skills, your emotional quotient all gets affected if you are not healthy. So there is no other alternative , keep health as your super-most priority in your to-do list and spare an hour or so engaging in activities which can lubricate your body, fuel it with right food, right exercise so that your thought process also gets right .

Early to bed, early to rise,
Keeps you healthy, wealthy and wise

But it is not crime if you are a night warrior but make sure you spare an hour from your regular time to play some sports, or engage in dance, 10–15 min of relaxation will help you de-stress yourself and if you can change your habit and start rising early you will do wonderfully well for sure.

Below are some simple and practical tips to help us overcome the problem:-

Start Your Day Early
Experience early morning beauty of our nature as it is universally proven that the best way to keep yourself healthy and energized is to start your day early and experience the beauty of God's creation while taking a walk for min 15–20 min (if weather allows). Feel the fresh air and greeneries around

you and remain present, you will have the best solo time being absorbed in the moment. Also morning hours gives you an opportunity to be social if you share your morning journey with your close friends or partner.

15 Minutes of Relaxation and Devotion
If you can invest 20 minutes daily on relaxation and relaxation keeping your gadget aside, it will prove to be your best investment decision. It will keep you in right shape and right frame of mind to make better decisions at your workplace. My personal relaxation includes deep abdominal breathing cycles for 5 minutes and my devotion involves reading or listening to audio Scriptures.

Be Emotionally Healthy
Everyone knows that if you are physically ill you need to consult your doctor, take medication and you will be alright. But few people actually give a damn if they are emotionally stressed, feeling low or depressed, we never consult or talk to specialist for it. Most of new generation leaders and successful entrepreneurs are fighting from depression; they feel isolated and do not speak their plight out. Sometimes they just need some dose of encouragement from the fellow human being but they hesitate to speak out about their weakness and want to present the better picture to the world outside, which is really very precarious.

Our emotional state has to be on a check especially when we are going through some issues that are traumatizing. It is always wise to go and consult as specialist, speak up to whom you trust, don't take all the burden alone, engage in more social activities instead of burning your energy on social media. Being emotionally fit should be the topmost priority if you are running your startup or any business for that matter. You need to invest your time in activities which bring smile on your face and relaxes your mind such hobby. It is proven that sparing and spending time with the family and loved ones becomes a major health booster; they are your true treasure. Proper time management involves giving and receiving love. Our emotional quotient (EQ) is boosted up by a healthy relationship as we become more empathic and caring with the people around us. Emotionally fit person gets larger acceptability in their workplace and society at large.

Addiction to Work

Work addiction, often called *workaholism*, is a real mental health condition. Like any other addiction, work addiction is the inability to stop the behavior. It often stems from a compulsive need to achieve status and success, or to escape emotional stress. Work addiction is often driven by job success. And it's common in people described as perfectionists or obsessed achievers. Much like someone with a drug addiction, a person with a work addiction achieves a "high" from working. This leads them to keep repeating the behavior that gives them this high. People with a work addiction may be unable to stop the behavior despite the negative ways it may affect their personal and social life, physical or mental health.

In a culture where hard work is praised and putting in overtime is often expected, it can be difficult to recognize work addiction. People with a work addiction will often justify their behavior by explaining why it is a good thing and can help them achieve success. They may simply appear committed to their job or the success of their projects. However, ambition and addiction are quite different. A person with a work addiction may engage in compulsive work to avoid other aspects of their life, like troubling emotional issues or personal crises. And similar to other addictions, the person may engage in the behavior unaware of the negative effects that the addiction is causing. Symptoms of a work addiction include:

- putting in long hours at the office, even when not needed

- losing sleep to engage in work projects or finish tasks

- being obsessed with work-related success

- having intense fear of failure at work or business

- having an attitude "if I do not do it, it's not going to be done"

- being paranoid about work-related performance

- disintegrating personal relationships because of work

- having a defensive attitude toward others about their work

- using work as a way to avoid relationships

- working to cope with feelings of guilt or depression

- working to avoid dealing with crises like death, divorce or financial trouble

Prioritize your health — for the sake of others, as you shift priorities, also remember to take care of yourself. *"You can't work productively in a creative and nuanced way for more than a certain number of hours per day — and you certainly can't do it without proper sleep, nutrition, and exercise,"* says Blair-Loy[iii]. "We live in a culture where work demands and deserves our undivided allegiance," she says. And that sort of devotion does have its benefits. "You feel challenged by your work; you're engaged by it; you're learning new things; and you have the opportunity to shape other people's careers. It's extremely rewarding," she says. But when you give all your attention to work, you eventually pay a steep price, according to Stewart Friedman[iv], professor of management at the Wharton School and author of *"Leading the Life You Want: Skills for Integrating Work and Life."* Working long hours, taking few vacations, and never truly being "off" — because of the ubiquity of digital devices — is "harmful to your relationships, your health, and also your productivity," he says. Here are some tips to help you overcome your addiction. Numerous studies show that people who prioritize their health — eating well, taking breaks and time off, and getting plenty of exercise — have more energy and better focus. Of course, warns

Friedman, "if you're [only] thinking about these things out of your own interest, it's not going to be sustainable." You must also think about the other people — clients, friends, coworkers, and family — who count on you and your good health. "That mindset changes your motivation," he says.

Principles to Remember
Do:
- Redefine personal success to be more about high-quality relationships, community engagement, physical and spiritual wellness.

- Be deliberate about how you choose to spend your time and with whom you spend it.

- Try mindfulness.

Don't:
- Go it alone — enlist colleagues, family, and friends to help you disengage.

- Automatically reach for your phone. whenever you have a down moment.

- Skimp on exercise, sleep, and wholesome food.

Low Self Esteem
Although some studies have demonstrated that individuals from lower socioeconomic groups have higher tendencies toward materialism, it is not known whether this association is causal, and the underlying psychological mechanisms are not

clear. Therefore, a study was conducted to examine the causal relationship between social class, materialism, and the role of self-esteem among Chinese college students. It was found that lower-class students had elevated self-esteem in the materialism. In other words these lower-class college students show high materialism tendencies to compensate for low self-esteem[v]. Low self-esteem and materialism go hand in hand as the joke goes about the bigger and redder the sports car, the smaller the self-esteem of the occupant. Researchers also demonstrated that low self-esteem and materialism are not just a correlation, but there is also an inversely proportional causal relationship between the two; where low self-esteem increases materialism, and inversely, materialism can also create low self-esteem. They also found that as self-esteem increases, materialism decreases. Even a simple gesture to raise self-esteem dramatically decreased materialism, which provides a way to cope with insecurity.

Whenever people experience a decline in self-esteem (and in many this condition is permanent), the stage is set for the use of material possessions as a coping strategy for feelings of low self-worth. The paradox that findings such as these bring up is that consumerism is good for the economy but bad for the individual. In the short run, it's good for the economy when people believe they need to buy an entirely new wardrobe every year, for example. But the hidden cost is much higher than the dollar amount. There are costs in mental health when people believe that their value is extrinsic and conditional. There are also environmental costs associated with widespread materialism and self-centeredness.

Most people want more income so they can consume more. Yet as societies become richer, they do not become happier. In fact, the First World has more depression, more alcoholism and more crime than fifty years ago. This paradox is true of Britain, the United States, continental Europe and Japan. Statistically people have more things than they did 50 years ago, but they are actually less happy in several key areas. There is also the considerable cost of what materialism does to the environment. We don't yet know what final toll that could take in terms of quality of life and overall happiness. What many people don't understand is that if we want to save the environment then we have to buy and consume less. We don't need to buy so much bottled water, for example. Studies have shown it is usually not any purer than city tap water, which doesn't leave mountains of plastic bottles strewn across the nation's landfills. It also wastes energy and resources to make those plastic bottles and the many other unnecessary things that both youth and adults alike believe they need to have in order to enjoy life and feel good about themselves.

Studies like this one miss the point by proceeding from the assumption that the reason people want whatever is currently "hot" is because they believe it will contribute towards their satisfaction and happiness in life. This is not the reason. It's not that people believe that buying more and more things will make them happy, (and in fact research has shown time and time again that this simply isn't the case.) It's that people live their lives terrified of what other people will think of them if they don't join in with the 'latest' trend.

Their self-esteem is entirely dependent on what others think of them. It's a form of enslavement, ruled by conditional regard, based at root on insecurity, and until the reasons are perceived no solution will be forthcoming.

When it comes to your self-worth, only one opinion truly matters — your own. And even that one should be carefully evaluated; we tend to be our own harshest critics. Dr. Glenn describes healthy self-esteem as a realistic, appreciative opinion of oneself. He writes, "Unconditional human worth assumes that each of us is born with all the capacities needed to live fruitfully, although everyone has a different mix of skills, which are at different levels of development." He emphasizes that core worth is independent of externals that the marketplace values, such as wealth, education, health, status — or the way one has been treated[vi].Some navigate the world — and relationships — searching for any bit of evidence to validate their self-limiting beliefs. Much like judge and jury, they constantly put themselves on trial and sometimes sentence themselves to a lifetime of self-criticism.

Following are eight steps you can take to increase your feelings of self-worth.

Be mindful
We can't change something if we don't recognize that there is something to change. By simply becoming aware of our negative self-talk, we begin to distance ourselves from the feelings it brings up. This enables us to identify with them less. Without this awareness, we can easily fall into the

trap of believing our self-limiting talk, and as it is said, *"Don't believe everything you think. Thoughts are just that — thoughts."* As soon as you find yourself going down the path of self-criticism, gently note what is happening, and remind yourself, "These are thoughts, not facts."

Change the story.
We all have a narrative or a story we've created about ourselves that shapes our self-perceptions, upon which our core self-image is based. If we want to change that story, we have to understand where it came from and where we received the messages we tell ourselves. Whose voices are we internalizing? "Sometimes automatic negative thoughts like 'you're fat' or 'you're lazy' can be repeated in your mind so often that you start to believe they are true," says Jessica Koblenz,. "These thoughts are learned, which means they can be unlearned. You can start with affirmations. What do you wish you believed about yourself? Repeat these phrases to yourself every day."

Dr. Thomas Boyce supports the use of affirmations. Research conducted by Boyce and his colleagues has demonstrated that "fluency training" in positive affirmations (for example, writing down as many different positive things you can about yourself in a minute) can lessen symptoms of depression as measured by self-report using the Beck Depression Inventory. Larger numbers of written positive statements are correlated with greater improvement. "While they have a bad reputation because of late-night TV," Boyce says, "positive affirmations can help."

Avoid falling into the compare-and-despair rabbit hole.

"Two key things I emphasize are to practice acceptance and stop comparing yourself to others," says psychotherapist Kimberly Hershenson, "I emphasis that just because someone else appears happy on social media or even in person doesn't mean they are happy. Comparisons only lead to negative self-talk, which leads to anxiety and stress." Feelings of low self-worth can negatively affect your mental health as well as other areas in your life, such as work, relationships, and physical health.

Channel your inner rock star

Albert Einstein said, "Everybody is a genius. But if you judge a fish by its ability to climb a tree, it will live its whole life believing that it is stupid." We all have our strengths and weaknesses. Someone may be a brilliant musician, but a dreadful cook. Neither quality defines their core worth. Recognize what your strengths are and the feelings of confidence they engender, especially in times of doubt. It's easy to make generalizations when you "mess up" or "fail" at something, but reminding yourself of the ways you rock offers a more realistic perspective of yourself. Psychotherapist Kristie Overstreet suggests asking yourself, "Was there a time in your life where you had better self-esteem? What were you doing at that stage of your life?" If it's difficult for you to identify your unique gifts, ask a friend to point them out to you. Sometimes it's easier for others to see the best in us than it is for us to see it in ourselves.

Exercise

Many studies have shown a correlation between exercise and higher self-esteem, as well as improved mental health. "Exercising creates empowerment both physical and mental," says Debbie Mandel, author of Addicted to Stress, "especially weight lifting where you can calibrate the accomplishments. Exercise organizes your day around self-care." She suggests dropping a task daily from your endless to-do list for the sole purpose of relaxation or doing something fun, and seeing how that feels. Other forms of self-care, such as proper nutrition and sufficient sleep, have also been shown to have positive effects on one's self-perception.

Do unto others.

Hershenson suggests volunteering to help those who may be less fortunate. "Being of service to others helps take you out of your head. When you are able to help someone else, it makes you less focused on your own issues." Dr. David Simonsen agrees, "What I find is that the more someone does something in their life that they can be proud of, the easier it is for them to recognize their worth. Doing things that one can respect about themselves is the one key that I have found that works to raise one's worth. It is something tangible. Helping at a homeless shelter, animal shelter, giving of time at a big brother or sister organization. These are things that mean something and give value to not only oneself, but to someone else as well."

There is much truth to the fact that what we put out there into the world tends to boomerang back to us. To test this out, spend a day intentionally putting out positive thoughts and behaviors toward those with whom you come into contact. As you go about your day, be mindful of what comes back to you, and also notice if your mood improves.

Forgiveness
Is there someone in your life you haven't forgiven? An ex-partner? A family member? Yourself? By holding on to feelings of bitterness or resentment, we keep ourselves stuck in a cycle of negativity. If we haven't forgiven ourselves, shame will keep us in this same loop. "Forgiving self and others has been found to improve self-esteem," says Schiraldi, "perhaps because it connects us with our innately loving nature and promotes an acceptance of people, despite our flaws."

Remember that you are not your circumstances.
Finally, learning to differentiate between your circumstances and who you are is key to self-worth. "Recognizing inner worth, and loving one's imperfect self, provides the secure foundation for growth," says Schiraldi. "With that security, one is free to grow with enjoyment, not fear of failure — because failure doesn't change core worth." We are all born with infinite potential and equal worth as human beings. That we are anything less is a false belief that we have learned over time. Therefore, with hard work and self-compassion, self-destructive thoughts and beliefs can be unlearned. Taking the steps outlined above is a start in the effort to increase self-worth, or as Schiraldi says, to "recognize self-worth. It already exists in each person."

Wealth and Life Purpose

Money is simply a tool to help you fulfill your life's purpose! Think of any other possession you have that would be considered a tool. Saws help us cut things. Washers and dryers help us clean your clothes while reliable vehicles help us get from point A to point B with ease and safety. Places to live in a house or apartment are simply tools to help us meet our basic survival needs of shelter, but also if planned right increase our creature comfort as well. Computers, cell phones, laptops are in our lives to make life more efficient. These are all tools that simply help us achieve a goal or solve a problem. At issue are some very important concepts regarding tools. The user manuals do not make one an expert tool handle only by proper use can one become expert in handling tools for his or her benefit. All tools need proper care and maintenance to work properly. If handled properly, they are a blessing but if handled improperly, they are a curse and can become burdensome.

So it is with money—Money is simply a tool and if we started looking at the money this way, we will get less stressed over money. One needs to become an expert at handling this tool his or her benefit. It really is that simple, the first thing we need to know is what it is that this tool called money is supposed to do for us.

Wealth needs to be maintained and backed up by a bigger purpose in life. Core values creation helps us not to veer off course.

> *"Don't tell me where your priorities are. Show me where you spend your money and I'll tell you what they are."*
> —*James W. Frick*

Enjoy the journey since you might not reach the destination. The process of wealth accumulation brings about new disciplines, new relationships, new knowledge, new ideas, and new way of thinking. It is advisable to enjoy the new you and celebrate each moment and achieve along the way.
Life is shorter than you think so live if fully today and add value in others; that brings more satisfaction than material accumulation.

Henry David Thoreau (American essayist and philosopher) wrote, *"Wealth is the ability to fully experience life"*. Wealth, its creation, utilization, and accumulation, is a very subjective matter and the truth is no matter how much wealth we accumulate, it never ceases to be enough.

Personal Core Values List by Category

Integrity
Accountability
Candor
Commitment
Dependability
Dignity
Honesty
Honor
Responsibility
Sincerity
Transparency
Trust
Trustworthy
Truth

Feelings
Acceptance
Comfort
Compassion
Contentment
Empathy
Grace
Gratitude
Happiness
Hope
Inspiring
Irreverent
Joy
Kindness
Love
Optimism
Passion
Peace
Poise
Respect
Reverence
Satisfaction
Serenity
Thankful
Tranquility
Welcoming

Spirituality
Adaptability
Altruism
Balance
Charity
Communication
Community
Connection
Consciousness

Contribution
Cooperation
Courtesy
Devotion
Equality
Ethical
Fairness
Family
Fidelity
Friendship
Generosity
Giving
Goodness
Harmony
Humility
Loyalty
Maturity
Meaning
Selfless
Sensitivity
Service
Sharing
Spirit
Stewardship
Support
Sustainability
Teamwork
Tolerance
Unity

Achievement
Accomplishment
Capable
Challenge
Challenge
Competence
Credibility
Determination
Development
Drive
Effectiveness
Empower
Endurance
Excellence
Famous
Greatness
Growth
Hard work
Improvement
Influence
Intensity

Leadership
Mastery
Motivation
Performance
Persistence
Potential
Power
Productivity
Professionalism
Prosperity
Recognition
Results-oriented
Risk
Significance
Skill
Skillfulness
Status
Success
Talent
Victory
Wealth
Winning

Creativity
Creation
Curiosity
Discovery
Exploration
Expressive
Imagination
Innovation
Inquisitive
Intuitive
Openness
Originality
Uniqueness
Wonder

Enjoyment
Amusement
Enthusiasm
Experience
Fun
Playfulness
Recreation
Spontaneous
Surprise

Presence
Alertness
Attentive
Awareness
Beauty
Calm
Clear
Concentration
Focus
Silence
Simplicity
Solitude

Intelligence
Brilliance
Clever
Common sense
Decisiveness
Foresight
Genius
Insightful
Knowledge
Learning
Logic
Openness
Realistic
Reason
Reflective
Smart
Thoughtful
Understanding
Vision
Wisdom

Strength
Ambition
Assertiveness
Boldness
Confidence
Dedication
Discipline
Fortitude
Persistence
Power
Restraint
Rigor
Self-reliance
Temperance
Toughness
Vigor
Will

Freedom	**Order**	Lawful	**Health**
Independence	Accuracy	Moderation	Energy
Individuality	Careful	Organization	Vitality
Liberty	Certainty	Security	
	Cleanliness	Stability	
Courage	Consistency	Structure	
Bravery	Control	Thorough	
Conviction	Decisive	Timeliness	
Fearless	Economy		
Valor	Justice		

[i]Scott Jeffrey, Leadership and Business Coach, https://scottjeffrey.com/

[ii]By John Brandon "6 Signs You are Sacrificing Too Much for Success" Contributing editor, Inc.com. https://www.inc.com/john-brandon/6-signs-youre-sacrificing-too-much-for-success.html

[iii]Mary Blair-Loy, a sociologist and the founding director of the Center for Research on Gender in the Professions at the University of California, San Diego

[iv]Stewart Friedman, professor of management at the Wharton School and author of Leading the Life You Want: Skills for Integrating Work and Life

[v]Jing Lia, Mengxi Lua, Ting Xiaaand Yongyu Guo (2018). "Materialism as compensation for self-esteem among lower-class students" *Journal of Personality and Individual Differences*Volume 131, 1 Sept 2018, Pages 191-196

[vi]Glenn R. Schiraldi, Ph.D, author of The Self-Esteem WorkbookISBN: 9781572242524

four

Why Become Wealthy?

"We make a living by what we get, but we make a life by what we give."

—*Winston Churchill*

O ne day a very wealthy father took his son on a trip to the country for the sole purpose of showing his son how it was to be poor. They spent a few days and nights on the farm of what would be considered a very poor family. After their return from the trip, the father asked his son how he liked the trip. 'It was great, Dad,' the son replied. 'Did you see how poor people can be?' the father asked. 'Oh Yeah,' said the son. "'So what did you learn from the trip?' asked the father. The son answered, 'I saw that we have one dog and they had four. We have a pool that reaches to the middle of our garden and they have a river that has no end.'""We have imported lanterns and tube lights in our garden and they have the stars at night. Our patio reaches to the front yard and they have the whole horizon. We have a small piece of land to live on and they have fields that go beyond our sight. We have servants who serve us, but they serve others.'"

"'We buy our food, but they grow theirs. We have walls around our property to protect us; they have friends to protect them." The boy's father was speechless. Then his son added, 'It showed me just how poor we really are.'"

Too many times we forget what we have and concentrate on what we don't have. What is one person's worthless object is another's prize possession. It is all based on one's perspective. Sometimes it takes the perspective of a child to remind us what's important. Dan Asmussen shared this story on social media and went viral and challenged me to think again about how I view life and possession.

Types of Blessings

What is Blessing?

Essentially, blessing is God giving power to something or somebody to do that which they are designed or intended to do. The creatures were supposed to fill the earth and multiply and so God gave them his blessing. Human beings were also supposed to multiply numerically, but also to take care of the rest of creation, and God gave them power to do that too. Blessing is God granting the power to do what he wants us and intends us to do and become[i].

There are two categories of blessings that we will limit ourselves in this discussion; the *Physical or Bodily Blessings* and the *Spiritual or Intangible Blessings*.

Physical (Bodily) Blessings

This pertains to our body and includes physical

needs such as food, water, shelter, clothing, good health, good environment and all that pertains to our safe and secure life.

Spiritual (Intangible) Blessings
This pertains to our soul, mind and spiritual being. This will include all intangible and perceived things such as freedom to worship without interference, availability and access to knowledge that is problem-solving, relevant and practical, ability to relate freely socially and express and receive love at all levels.

> *"Don't just count your blessings. Be the blessing other people count on."*
> —*Anonymous*

Charity and Donations
The virtue of charity means being generous with our presence, time and money as charity allows us to give freely without expecting anything in return. Charity is an essential sign of faith as both Jewish and Christian ethics are built upon charitable acts and deeds. The virtue of charity encompasses a range of small acts and habits that affects our own immediate surroundings as well as the larger global community. It can be as simple as giving someone a smile or it can be expressed on a larger scale through raising funds for world organizations such as Development and Peace or Free the Children.

It applies not just to our personal relationships with other people, but also extends to things, animals, plants, and the Earth. All creation is interrelated. Charity allows us to see how we are connected to others through time and space. We have a responsibility to nurture, support, and be in solidarity with those around us.

Importance of Giving

A friend of mine had this idea that millionaires ought to give more and help others through charities because they have more. Most of us might have this way of thinking and it is logical that if you have more you ought to give more and if you have nothing then you are exempt from giving to others. This way of looking at things has flaws because it undermines the fact that everybody has something that somebody needs. We live in the global village where there is lots of wastage in one part of the globe while the other side suffers scarcity. If we will lift our eyes and look beyond our homes, neighborhoods, villages, borders and boundaries we will quickly see the need beyond the fence and we will become a solution to many problems and an answer to somebody's prayer.

One Jewish teacher said "the poor will be with you forever". We do not have to look very hard to find somebody who is needy and our extended hand would make a difference. I strongly believe that the wealthy are so because they give more and the poor remain so because they only receive. There is what is called a *Principle of Reciprocity*, what you do to others it will be done to you. Others call it the Boomerang Effect, —the Ancient Scriptures say "The generous soul will be made rich; he who waters others shall himself be watered....."[ii]

Giving back to society is in fact vague and

misty in nature. There's so much that we procure from society. There are so many strata of people who make up the whole population of a nation. But they are different from each other. Some are affluent and some are mere strugglers of survival. In many countries, there are masses who don't even have excess to basic day-to-day requirements. There are also people who have so much in excess, that the amounts if distributed would solve many problems plaguing most areas around the world.

> *Man should not consider his material possession his own, but as common to all, so as to share them without hesitation when others are in need.*
> —*Thomas Aquinas*

Benefits of Giving

Giving makes us happy and healthier

There have been many studies about the happiness level of people who gave money to charities or volunteered their time. Across the board, these studies always seem to point at the happiness of people who give. It was found in a 2002 survey by the National Opinion Research Center's General Social Survey that 43 percent of people who gave blood two or three times a year were very happy, as opposed to the 29 percent who didn't.

A 2008 study by Harvard Business School professor Michael Norton and colleagues found that giving money to someone else lifted participants' happiness more than spending it on themselves (despite participants' prediction that spending on themselves would make them happier). Happiness expert Sonja Lyubomirsky, a professor of psychology at the University of California, Riverside, saw similar results when she asked people to perform five acts of kindness each week for six weeks. These good feelings are reflected in our biology. In a 2006 study, Jorge Moll and colleagues at the National Institutes of Health found that when people give to charities, it activates regions of the brain associated with pleasure, social connection, and trust, creating a "warm glow" effect. Scientists also believe that altruistic behavior releases endorphins in the brain, producing the positive feeling known as the "helper's high." One contributing aspect to cycles of depression is the feeling of isolation. Studies have shown that volunteering and giving to others helps combat self-hatred and mental illness[iii].

Giving helps us live longer
The journal Health Psychology published a study in 2012 that found people who regularly volunteer live longer. But there was a catch—it had to be for unselfish reasons. If you volunteered for any reason beyond the joy of giving, it didn't have the same long-term health benefits[iv]. A wide range of research has linked different forms of generosity to better health, even among the sick and elderly. In his book *Why Good Things Happen to Good People*, Stephen Post, a professor of preventative medicine at Stony Brook University, reports that giving to others has been shown to increase health benefits in people with chronic illness, including HIV and multiple sclerosis.

A 1999 study led by Doug Oman of the University of California, Berkeley, found that elderly people who volunteered for two or more organizations were 44 percent less likely to die over a five-year period than were non-volunteers, even after controlling for their age, exercise habits, general health, and negative health habits like smoking. Stephanie Brown of the University of Michigan saw similar results in a 2003 study on elderly couples. She and her colleagues found that those individuals who provided practical help to friends, relatives, or neighbors, or gave emotional support to their spouses, had a lower risk of dying over a five-year period than those who didn't. Interestingly, receiving help wasn't linked to a reduced death risk. Researchers suggest that one reason giving may improve physical health and longevity is that it helps decrease stress, which is associated with a variety of health problems. In a 2006 study by Rachel Piferi of Johns Hopkins University and Kathleen Lawler of the University of Tennessee, people who provided social support to others had lower blood pressure than participants who didn't, suggesting a direct physiological benefit to those who give of themselves.

Giving gives our life meaning
Sean Stannard-Stockton is an investment advisor, regularly consults with wealthy individuals about how to maximize the financial resources at their disposal. He specializes in working with philanthropic families, and that work often lays bare the seeming conflict between maximizing resources and giving them away. If humans want to maximize the resources available to them, why do they take such joy in giving these resources away? He believes that giving is motivated by humans'

deeply held need to find meaning in life. For most people, meaning is deeply intertwined with community connections (defining community as narrowly as family and as broadly as the full community of life). Humans want to feel a sense of connection and a sense of purpose to life. Giving (time, money, and energy) is a central way that we strive to find meaning. Much has been made of selfish motivations behind giving. No doubt, some giving is motivated by selfishness. However, if we look to *Maslow's hierarchy* of needs (a central theory of what drives human behavior) we find that while humans are driven by items that benefit them, once these needs (shelter, food, clothing, sleep, security, etc.) are met, they are driven by the desire for self-actualization.

Maslow describes self-actualizing people as follows—

- They embrace the facts and realities of the world (including themselves) rather than denying or avoiding them.

- They are spontaneous in their ideas and actions.

- They are creative.

- They are interested in *solving problems*; this often includes the problems of others. Solving these problems is often a key focus in their lives.

- They feel a closeness to other people, and generally appreciate life.

- They have a system of morality that is fully internalized and independent of external authority.

They have discernment and are able to view all things in an objective manner.

To me, this is a wonderful description of the very best philanthropists. Because what is good for our community is good for each of us (individuals in thriving, happy communities are generally happier themselves), there is a way in which giving comes back to benefit the giver. This feedback loop is wonderful, but I believe that humans' motivation to give is rooted in their desire to find meaning through community, not the hope that doing so will benefit them.

Recently, much research has focused on how our brains are hardwired to chemically reward us for acts of giving. To some, the idea that giving would trigger this sort of response implies a level of selfishness behind the act of charity. But this logic implicitly suggests that breathing, eating, and falling in love are all "selfish" as well, since our brain chemistry rewards us in similar ways for these actions.

Rather than suggesting that giving is selfish, I think the research shows that giving is a central need and desire for humans. This is actually quite remarkable, since logic would dictate that giving is something we do for others, and that we must lose something for others to gain. Instead, the research suggests that giving is a motivation much like eating and breathing. It is something we must do to survive and thrive. The motivations of each individual giver are of course unique. But just as we eat to satisfy our desire to live, we give to satisfy our desire for meaning.

Giving increases our confidence
One critical element to a poor self-image is constant focus on ourselves and our state of being. Self-preoccupation breeds a false self-understanding while giving helps to move our focus away from us and on to others. It's great to have a strong sense of self-awareness, but that inner voice can be a constant force for criticism and negativity. Being generous not only changes where we're placing the spotlight, but it helps give our brain a positive argument for why we're not so bad. Helping someone else often enables us to forget about ourselves and to feel grateful for what we have. It also feels good when we are able to make a difference for someone else. Instead of focusing on our own weaknesses, volunteer to mentor, assist or teach another, and you'll see your self-confidence grow automatically in the process.

> *"Low self-esteem is like driving through life with your hand brake on."*
> —Maxwell Maltz

Being generous also makes us feel better about ourselves. Generosity is both a natural confidence builder and a natural repellant of self-hatred. By focusing on what we are giving rather than on what we are receiving, we create a more outward orientation toward the world, which shifts our focus away from ourselves. While maintaining a healthy level of self-awareness and sensitivity to oneself is important, too often we narrow in on ourselves with a negative lens. We spend too much time listening to the *"critical inner voice"* in our heads, which scrutinizes our every move and nags at us with negative thoughts towards ourselves and others. These negative thoughts undermine our confidence and can lead to self-sabotage. Being generous distracts us from the critical inner voice's barrage of nasty thoughts and creates a strong argument against it as well. When we see someone else benefiting from our kind actions, for instance, it is hard for the inner voice to argue that we are worthless.

Giving promotes cooperation and social connection. As stated earlier about the Principle of Reciprocity —*When we give, we are more likely to get back*: Several studies, including work by sociologists Brent Simpson and Robb Willer, have suggested that when you give to others, your generosity is likely to be rewarded by others down the line— sometimes by the person you gave to, sometimes by someone else. These exchanges promote a sense of trust and cooperation that strengthens our ties to others—and research has shown that having positive social interactions is central to good mental and physical health.

As researcher John Cacioppo writes in his book *Loneliness: Human Nature and the Need for Social Connection,* "The more extensive the reciprocal altruism born of social connection; the greater the advance toward health, wealth, and happiness."What's more, when we give to others, we don't only make them feel closer to us; we also feel closer to them. "Being kind and generous leads us to perceive others more positively and more charitably," writes Lyubomirsky in her book *The How of Happiness*, and this "fosters a heightened sense of interdependence and cooperation in our social community."

Giving evokes gratitude
Whether you're on the giving or receiving end of a gift, that gift can elicit feelings of gratitude—it can be a way of expressing gratitude or instilling gratitude in the recipient. And research has found that gratitude is integral to happiness, health, and social bonds. Robert Emmons and Michael McCullough, co-directors of the Research Project on Gratitude and Thankfulness, found that teaching college students to "count their blessings" and cultivate gratitude caused them to exercise more, be more optimistic, and feel better about their lives overall. A recent study led by Nathaniel Lambert at Florida State University found that expressing gratitude to a close friend or spouse strengthens our sense of connection to that person.

Barbara Fredrickson, a pioneering happiness researcher, suggests that cultivating gratitude in everyday life is one of the keys to increasing personal happiness. "When you express your gratitude in words or actions, you not only boost your own positivity but other people's as well," she writes in her book *Positivity*. "And in the process you reinforce their kindness and strengthen your bond to one another."

Giving is contagious
When we give, we don't only help the immediate recipient of our gift. We also spur a ripple effect of generosity through our friends and community at

large. A study by James Fowler of the University of California, San Diego, and Nicholas Christakis of Harvard, published in the Proceedings of the National Academy of Science, shows that when one person behaves generously, it inspires observers to behave generously too, toward different people. In fact, the researchers found that altruism could spread by three degrees—from person to person to person to person. "As a result," they write, "each person in a network can influence dozens or even hundreds of people, some of whom he or she does not know and has not met."

Giving has also been linked to the release of oxytocin, a hormone (also released during sex and breast feeding) that induces feelings of warmth, euphoria, and connection to others. In laboratory studies, Paul Zak, the director of the Center for Neuroeconomics Studies at Claremont Graduate University, has found that a dose of oxytocin will cause people to give more generously and to feel more empathy towards others, with "symptoms" lasting up to two hours. And those people on an "oxytocin high" can potentially jump-start a "virtuous circle, where one person's generous behavior triggers another's," says Zak.

Practicing Generosity

Give something that is sensitive
Generosity is most effective when the gift you offer is sensitive. Think about what the other person wants or needs. It's not always about material things; it's about being giving of yourself. Sometimes just being present and available to a loved one who is having a hard time is the greatest gift you could possibly give.

Accept appreciation.

It is important to be open to the people who express appreciation toward you. Generosity is a two-way street, allowing someone to express their gratitude is an important aspect of generosity and part of what makes you feel closer to them. As researchers in the Department of Psychology at University of North Carolina at Chapel Hill have discovered, "The emotion of gratitude uniquely functions to build a high-quality relationship between a grateful person and the target of his or her gratitude, that is, the person who performed a kind action." So it is important to not brush off a "thank you" with comments like "Oh, it was nothing."

Accept the generosity of others.

Some people have a much easier time being giving than receiving. However, it is important to let others do things for you. I call this the generosity of acceptance. Being pseudo-independent or self-denying robs your loved ones of the opportunity to feel the joy of giving. Accepting the generosity of others may make you uncomfortable if you felt unlovable or unworthy in your early life. Generosity is often an act of love, and though it may seem counterintuitive, many people respond negatively to being loved.

Show appreciation.

Remember that gratitude is an important part of the equation. Show your appreciation for the generosity that is directed toward you, even if you feel shy or uncomfortable. Resist the temptation to say things like "This is too much," or "You shouldn't have." Instead just say "Thank you!" Or, better yet, let the person know what their generosity meant to you. Generosity is truly the gift that keeps on giving.

Each day life presents us with hundreds of opportunities to be generous; by making a lifestyle out of generosity, we can do ourselves and others a world of good.

Become A Blessing

The sole reason that we are becoming wealthy and prosperous both in religious and psychological point of view is that we become a blessing to others. The very reason for our existence is to become part of each other and lead a life of interconnectedness. As discussed earlier, we are the conduit or the channel of goodness, kindness, happiness and love to others. Ancient Scriptures singles out a man called Abraham who was blessed for the only reason to become a *blessing* to the families of the earth. In his generation and time about 2000 BC he was considered wealthy and very prosperous because of his faith. Through him many promises of physical and spiritual blessings spill to the present generation through faith and carefully studying the principles he used to accomplish his life assignment.

Beyond Chinese Proverb

"You give a poor man a fish and you feed him for a day. You teach him to fish and you give him an occupation that will feed him for a lifetime."

Many foreign aid organizations have done a great job in helping 3rd world countries in times of catastrophes and disasters such as draught resulting to famine, civil wars, natural disasters, outbreaks etc. These foreign aid initiatives are very critical and imperative to get people from where they are to where they could stand on their feet. Unfortunately, some of these initiatives have created a vicious cycle of dependency and lack of accountability on the recipient side.

I believe there has to be a specific timeline and exit strategy on how to make these communities self-sustainable. Going back to the Chinese proverb; many times I have gone to ponds, lakes and ocean where I found the sign post saying *"NO FISHING"!* With increasing levels of unemployment and restrictions in communal resources, *I will suggest that we do not only teach poor people how to fish but how to farm the fish—aquaculture!*

This will solve lots of problems that are short term and create generational wealth. It is not only the question of survival with our families but to become a blessing to the families of the earth. A fisherman in 3rd world country barely supports his family but a fish farmer (Aquaculturist) supports the economy of the entire community and nation. I encourage individuals and organizations to rethink and revisit the charities that they provide to poor people worldwide by asking fundamental question—

What are we providing the poor and needy people? The more we think through and analyze our charity the better the results of our efforts.
We provide one of the following—
  • *Fish*

- *Fishing rod*

- *Fish farming*

Fish Based Charity

This is a temporary solution for the incident sometimes called a *Workaround*; it is essentially a temporary measure to reduce or eliminate the impact of an incident or a problem. It can be used to fix the issue the person is facing until a permanent solution can be implemented. They key concept here is *"temporary"* meaning that there has to be a clear timeframe, objectives, strategy and exit plan. There has to be a sense of accountability on both ends; the donor and recipient on how they will cooperate in solving the solution without creating another problem of chronic dependency on the recipient side.

In many world cultures it is taboo asking how they are going to spend the money and also an account of how the donation money has been spent. Members of the family get infuriated when asked to give an account on how the donated money designated for kid's surgery or education has been used. One organization taking care of orphans literally refused to take our donations on basis that *"we ask too much questions"* on how the donation funds are been used. Giving *Fish based charity* has a lot of challenges in terms of abuse of power and improper allocation of resources based on felt local needs.

I personally believe in string attachment to any donation where it is individual, national or multinational. The strings have to be the accountability factor and demonstration that it does not development unhealthy dependency to those targeted to be helped. However, most foreign aid to 3rd world is looked at suspicion because they ties that come with them are devious and evil. These foreign aid strings can be exploitative in nature and put these poor countries in worse condition than they were currently in. The major failure of many *governmental welfare programs* is to favor help with current consumption while placing almost no emphasis on job training or anything else that might allow today's poor people to become self-sufficient in the future. It is the classic example giving a man a fish and not teaching him how to fish. Government welfare programs hand out lots of fish, but never seem to teach people how to fish for themselves. Those in the welfare programs need to learn very quickly the dangers of consumption over investment of their time, resources, and ability.

Fishing Rod Based Charity
This is hypothetically the correct approach, for many years people talked about teaching the poor and need how to fish themselves. To best of the knowledge at that time it seemed beneficial and helped many families and even countries to be self-sustainable. However, self-sustainability should not the destination for any individual, family, community or nation; but wealth creation. Wealth is not created by learning how to fish and depend on somebody else to give you permission to fish on their pond or lake. You will always be dependent to who owns the fish pond and what quota is allocated to you. This is typical subsistence mindset, working for survival and making

ends meet or providing for the daily bread mentality.

Most of the world education system is based on training people to work for somebody else. We are training employees that will work in factories, industries and corporations that once they size down then these graduates will never have a life of their own. We were delusional to think that the education we were given was preparing us to become wealthy fish farmers, not just glorified hired fishermen who own nothing but a skill to fish. Get me right, I am not saying education is bad; what I say is if it does not prepare us to be owners and wealth generators then it is self-sabotaging, redundant and outdated. In the same vein our generosity has to follow the same guideline on what exactly do we want to achieve as we are assisting others.

Fish Farming Charity
This is the highest type of charity that makes a long lasting difference and impact from individual to national level. It is termed as "blessings of destiny" because they solve the present and future problems by looking deep as the root cause. This is a practical and holistic approach to issues around poverty and wealth generation based on the principle of causation. Here we teach people how to farm the fish and own the ponds or portions of lakes and oceans to feed themselves, their communities and the nations.

This is a more sustainable approach to wealth generation and not only survive but thrive to become a blessing to the families of the earth. Fish farmers not only feed the nations but create employment, preserve the environment, contribute significantly to the national economy literally and figuratively. We need to switch our mindset as we assist others to make them not only job takers but job creators and givers. Most of 3rd world countries have lots of natural endowment of resources; if taught how to utilize them these countries will not only be self-sustainable but wealthy enough to support other countries.

This mindset generates a ripple effect to others in the community who are helped also to know how to generate wealth that will be useful to help others too. Before we realize we will become a blessing to the families of the earth since we won't only help one person but the entire community and a nation as a whole. This phenomenon is termed *blessing of destiny* as coined by Bishop Bismark Tudor, the senior pastor of New Life Covenant Church of Harare, Zimbabwe. It changes the destiny of individuals, families, communities and societies at large.

The Tale of Two Seas

Dorothy my wife and I decided to have a tour in the Middle East during Easter of 2018. Sitting in the presentations many times people talked of Dead Sea and I could not wait to visit the site and experience it fast hand. We were fascinated to learn and experience that the Dead Sea is so high in salt content that the human body can float easily; you do not need to know how to swim to enjoy the buoyancy of the water. We were surprised that there were no lifeguards only few volunteers to help people clean salty water from their eyes! You can almost lie down and read a book! The salt in the Dead Sea is as high as 35% —almost 10 times the normal ocean water. And all that saltiness has meant that there is no life at all in the Dead Sea. Absolutely no fish, vegetation or sea animals can survive that level of salinity and virtually nothing lives in the Dead Sea—and hence the name *Dead Sea.*

While the Dead Sea has remained etched in my memory, I don't seem to recall hearing about the Sea of Galilee in my school Geography lesson or people's presentations. So when we heard about the Sea of Galilee and the Dead Sea and the tale of the two seas— we were intrigued. It turns out that the Sea of Galilee is just north of the Dead Sea and both seas receive their water from river Jordan and yet they are very different. Unlike the Dead Sea, the Sea of Galilee is pretty, resplendent with rich, colorful marine life and lots of plants. In fact, the Sea of Galilee is home to over twenty different types of fishes. Same region, same source of water, and yet while one sea is full of life, the other is dead—How come? The River Jordan flows into the Sea of Galilee and then flows out and its waters simply passes through the Sea of Galilee in and then out—and that keeps the Sea healthy and vibrant, teeming with marine life. But the Dead Sea is so far below the mean sea level, that it has no outlet. The water flows in from the river Jordan, but does not flow out—*There are no outlet streams.* It is estimated that over a million tons of water evaporate from the Dead Sea every year leaving it salty, full of minerals and unfit for any marine life.

The Dead Sea takes water from the River Jordan, *and holds it not giving it away*—Resulting in lack of life whatsoever. Life is not just about getting but it is about giving as well and we all need to be a bit like the Sea of Galilee. We are fortunate to get wealth, knowledge, love and respect. But if we do not learn to give, we could all end up like the Dead Sea. The love and the respect, the wealth and the knowledge could all evaporate like the water in the Dead Sea and have no life in us that benefits others. If we get the *Dead Sea mentality* of merely taking in more water, more money, more everything the results can be disastrous. Good idea to make sure that in the sea of your own life, you have outlets. We need many outlets for love, wealth and everything else that we get in our life. We should make sure that we do not just get, but we also give too.

Wealth Generation
While world-class thinkers understand the importance of saving and investing, they direct their mental energy toward accumulating wealth through serving people and solving problems," writes self-made millionaire Steve Siebold in *"How Rich People Think,"* which he wrote after studying millionaires for over 25 years. The one greatest strategy of generation of wealth is becoming a solution to mankind and humanity. People are willing to exchange and trade whatever they have to solve the problem.

How Do You Solve the Problem?
I have suggested a seven-step process that we can use to solve the problem in order to generate wealth in a win-win approach.

Step 1: Recognize a problem exists.
We need to be conscious that the problem is present before we can figure out and accurately define what that problem is. Sometimes this is easier

said than done. It's easy to get complacent, to just accept that this is "the way things are". For instance, you might be unhappy with your financial situation; you might realize that something with the way you're handling money isn't working.

Step 2: Identify the problem.
After you've recognized that things aren't right, ask yourself why. What is the specific problem that's leading to your unhappiness? Is there more than one problem? Using the previous example, once you've realized you need to do something different with your dollars, you might find that debt is dragging you down. Sometimes it may be unplanned expenditures.

Step 3: Diagnose the source of the problem.
Next, try to figure out why your problem exists. How did it start? Why does it continue? Why does it make you unhappy? With our financial example, you'd quickly discover that your debt exists because you spend more than you earn. But why do you spend more than you earn? When did you start doing this? Why do you continue to do so?

Step 4: Brainstorm solutions.
Now that you've identified the problem (and its source), it's time to figure out how to fix things. This is the fun part. Come up with a list of ways you can overcome the problem that's been holding you back. To get out of debt, for instance, you might take a two-pronged approach: boost your income by taking a second job while also cutting back temporarily on some non-essentials.

Step 5: Formulate a plan.

Once you've come up with a solution to your problem, make a plan to turn these dreams into reality. How specifically are you going to implement your solution? What steps can you take today and tomorrow to solve the problem? If you're trying to trim your budget, you might draft a prioritized list of places you can cut your spending. Then you can write down concrete steps to take toward each of these goals.

Step 6: Take action.

This step is the most important. To solve any problem, you must take action. It doesn't do any good to identify the problem, to brainstorm solutions, and to formulate a plan if you're not going to do the work necessary to make things right. You'll never get out of debt if all you do is tell yourself you ought to spend less. You must truly spend less in order to eliminate the problem.

Step 7: Monetize your solution for public use.

Many people have good inventions and innovations that are buried in their backyards. These innovative systems are not presented to the public to solve everybody else's problems but the innovator and his immediate family.

History books ascertain that Thomas Edison was not the first person to invent the light bulb, but he was the first to bring to the market the prototype that was commercially practical and make his innovation of use to the public.

Facts about Generating Wealth

Guiding principles to generating wealth have to be ethical, legal and rational; since our pursuit to a wealthy lifestyle involves other people's wellbeing and interaction. We do not live in isolation, we are all bundled together and true wealth generation has to consider others while observing the golden rule—treat others as you would wish to be treated. In the following chapters, we will discuss five principles of generating wealth especially in the economical aspect in the more accelerated fashion

Investment versus Spending
There is a major the difference between spending and investing. Spending is a more-or-less even trade of money for goods and/or services, while investing is using your money to attract more money. In the culture of instant gratification where we want to satisfy our appetite for stuff today at the expense of tomorrow; makes investment a far off concept for many people. We spend more than we earn, and if we examine the things we spend most of our money to get are stuff that are of no use or somebody called them "adult toys".

In order to generate wealth we have to develop a culture of investment. Whatever we earn the major chunk of it has to go into investments and smaller percentile remains for us to spend. The rule of the thumb to whether we are spending or investing is to check if the money goes into assets or liabilities. Secondly, to be sure that we are not focusing too much on consumable stuff that has nothing to do with our future.
In just five years, Grant Cardone of Grant of Millennial Money went from having $2.26 in his bank account to $1 million. On his blog, the 31-year-

old self-made millionaire shares *"the single most important hack"* he's used to build wealth: "I break down ALL of my money goals into daily goals. I still deposit money every day into my investment accounts." He started with the goal of setting aside $50 a day. At first, "some days it was only $5, but I rarely missed a day," Grant says. "Then I started trying to make as much money as possible every day so I could invest it. I stopped thinking long term and thought every day about making that $50 threshold." His daily goal of $50 deposits soon became his daily minimum. He started setting aside $70, then $80, then $100 dollars a day. Then as my side hustles started really taking off I started depositing $500 or more a day. Then I put $5,000 in a day, then $20,000, and the rest is history."

Multiple Streams of Passive Income
Most people only have one stream of income and that source is usually receiving a salary or wages from working a job. This puts you in a risky financial situation because if that stream of income goes away you are in trouble, especially if you do not have a sizeable cash reserve. This is also the hardest way to earn income and is known as active income because you are trading your time for money. To be safe I recommend trying to develop at least three streams of income. This can come in the form of salaries, wages, investment income and income from side businesses you are involved in. If you observe wealthy people you will notice that many of them have over 5 or more sources of income. Many of them are involved in multiple businesses, have strong investment portfolios and

are usually the principal owner of a business they started or moved up in. This is known as passive income and is the best scenario to be in. Earning more investment income than income from your salary and side business is the ultimate goal because you are having your money work for you. You are no longer trading your time and effort for money.

Develop multiple streams of passive income "You won't get rich without multiple flows of income," says self-made millionaire Grant Cardone, who was deep in debt before reaching seven figures. That starts with the income you currently have. Increase that income and start adding multiple flows. "You want what are called symbiotic flows. Do not just add disconnected flows, instead, find other ways you can add income to the job you already have. My video guy does advertising for me — and after proving himself, he started making advertisements for those connected to me. He didn't start a doughnut shop; this connects to the *Leverage* discussed below.

Leverage
In principle, a lever allows you to use less force to lift or move objects. Leverage is an idea which humans have used to great effect for thousands of years, enabling them to gain disproportionate strength. For example, the ancient Egyptians used levers to lift stones weighing up to 100 tons in order to build the pyramids and obelisks. Many of humanity's tools, used for centuries all over the world, incorporate levers- scissors, pliers, door handles, wheelbarrows, fishing rods and more.

With regards to wealth generation, we can

likewise use the principle of leverage to accelerate our financial goals. When properly understood and intelligently applied, leveraging will allow us to earn more with less work. Building wealth requires us to work smarter rather than harder by applying the following principles of leverage:

- *Financial Leverage*: Other people's money so that you are not limited by your own pocketbook.

- *Asset Leverage:* Using existing assets to multiply their use for income generation.

- *Time Leverage*: Other people's time so that you are not limited to 24 hours in a day.

- *Systems and Technology Leverage*: Other people's or your existing systems and technology so that you can get more done with less effort.

- *Marketing Leverage:* Other people's magazines, newsletters, radio shows, and databases so that you can communicate to millions with no more effort than is required to communicate one-on-one.

- *Network Leverage*: Other people's resources and connections so that you can expand beyond your own.

- *Knowledge Leverage*: Other people's talents, expertise, and experience so that you can utilize greater knowledge than you will ever possess.

Leverage allows you to build more wealth than you could ever achieve alone by utilizing resources that extend beyond your own. It allows you to grow wealth without being restricted by your personal limitations. Leverage is built on the notion that small, well-focused actions can sometimes produce significant, enduring improvements if they are applied in the right place. Tacking a difficult problem is often a matter of seeing where the high leverage lies. A leverage point is where a small difference can make a large difference. Leverage points provide kernel ides and procedures for formulating solutions. Identifying leverage points helps us to create new courses of action, develop increased awareness of those things that may cause a difficult before there are any obvious signs of trouble and figure out what is causing a difficult[v].

Generating financial wealth can be reduced to a simple method: *solve a problem*. Figuring out an easy, quick, and profitable solution to a *ubiquitous* issue is the basic equation that any business follows. Either being the first to devise a solution, or coming in afterward to improve upon it — this is how entrepreneurs with simple ideas turn their concepts into successful companies.

[i] Genesis 1:22-28 Holy Bible

[ii] Proverbs 11:25-26 Holy Bible

[iii] Musick MA and Wilson J (2003) Volunteering and depression: the role of psychological and social resources in different age groups. Soc Sci Med. 2003 Jan;56(2):259-69.

[iv] Konrath, Sara Fuhrel-Forbis, Andrea Lou, Alina and Brown, Stephanie (2012). Motives for volunteering are associated with mortality risk in older adults. *https://psycnet.apa.org/record/2011-17888*

[v] Alan C. McLucas (2003). Decision Making: Risk Management, Systems Thinking, and Situation Awareness. ISBN 978-0958023825 Paperback: 232 pages Publisher: Argos Press; 1st edition

five

Personal Financial Skills and Literacy

"Stop chasing the money and start chasing the passion."

— Tony Hsieh

Oprah Winfrey was born into a poor Mississippi family in 1954, but that didn't stop her from achieving unparalleled success. After a traumatic upbringing in which she was abused and molested by two family members and a family friend, she ran away from home at the age of 13. At 14, she gave birth —the child died shortly after. Always an intelligent and driven young woman, Winfrey was awarded a scholarship to Tennessee State University. Following an appearance in a local beauty pageant, she went on to become the first African-American TV correspondent in the state at the young age of 19. The acclaimed talk show host later moved to Chicago, where she began work on her very own morning show. It would later be widely known as The Oprah Winfrey Show. The show aired for 25 seasons, from 1986 to 2011. Since moving on from her talk show, Winfrey has founded OWN, the Oprah Winfrey Network. Her net worth is calculated to be about $2.6 billion, making her one of the richest black women in the world.

Before he was the mastermind behind shampoo giant John Paul Mitchell Systems and Patron Tequila, John Paul DeJoria was just a first-generation American trying to make it. After his German and Italian parents divorced when he was two, he turned to selling Christmas cards and newspapers to help support his family — all before he turned 10 years old. After taking a job in a Redken factory, DeJoria became intrigued in the shampoo industry. He took a $700 loan from the company and invested it into his own brand, John Paul Mitchell Systems. Going door-to-door selling his product, DeJoria slept in his car, hoping his product would capture buyers' attention. It did — the company is now worth over $900 million annually. DeJoria has a net worth of $2.6 billion.

Abramovich was born in southern Russia, into poverty. After being orphaned at age 2, he was raised by an uncle and his family in a subarctic region of northern Russia. While a student at the Moscow Auto Transport Institute in 1987, he started a small company producing plastic toys, which helped him eventually found an oil business and make a name for himself within the oil industry. Later, as sole leader of the Sibneft company, he completed a merger that made it the fourth biggest oil company in the world. The company was sold to state-run gas titan Gazprom in 2005 for $13 billion. He acquired the Chelsea Football (Soccer) Club in 2003 and owns the world's largest yacht, which cost him almost $400 million in 2010, and he currently boosts of the net worth of 8.2 billion.

Born into a nomadic tribe in the Syrian desert to a poor mother who was raped by his father and died when he was young, Altrad was raised by his grandmother, who banned him from attending school, in Raqqa. Altrad attended school anyway, and when he moved to France to attend university, he knew no French and lived off of one meal a day. Still, he earned a PhD in computer science, worked for some leading French companies, and eventually bought a failing scaffolding company, which he transformed into one of the world's leading manufacturers of scaffolding and cement mixers, Altrad Group. He has previously been named French Entrepreneur of the Year and World Entrepreneur of the Year with more than 1 billion net worth.

Personal Finance Skills

Financial acumen at a basic level is possessing a solid understanding of what drives your earnings and expenses and how key financial metrics are used. You don't have to be a financial whiz, but you need financial acumen to:

- Understand and set your personal financial goals

- Recognize what actions need to be taken to improve your personal finance management

- Determine how to help yourself make more money, save more money and improve those key metrics used in tracking efficiency

You also need financial acumen so you can contribute more in meetings, hold strategic conversations and manage your finances with professionals who you hire to help you manage your finances. Marina Theodotou[i] of the American Management Association says that "strengthening your financial acumen is a must in today's economy." Mastering basic personal finance skills is one of the most important things you can do to improve your happiness and quality of life. The earlier you start developing and using personal finance skills, the more time you have to reap the benefits.

> *"Let others lead small lives, but not you. Let others argue over small things, but not you. Let others cry over small hurts, but not you. Let others leave their future in someone else's hands, but not you."*
>
> —*Jim Rohn*

There are twelve personal finance skills every frugal person should master according to Dr. Penny Pincher[ii]. Here are few that are important:-

Budgeting
Setting and following a budget is probably the most basic personal finance skill, yet only about one-third of people actually have a detailed budget. I personally went for years without a budget; using my paycheck and account balance as a rough gauge of how much money I had available to spend. Many individuals do that and it is a terrible way to run your personal finances. A detailed budget is necessary to get a handle on

where your money is going and to start deciding where you want your money to go — instead of just watching it go away! It is as simple as writing out a list of all of your income and expenses; this is the first step toward becoming skilled at budgeting. You need to monitor spending and work to stay on track every month. Sometimes unexpected expenses will pop up, and it takes skill to find ways to spend less in other areas to recover and stay on budget. You can get a real budget started by looking at your bank statements and credit card bills from last month and adding up spending by category. I used colored highlighters to mark up my spending into categories such as food, clothing, pets, entertainment, transportation, housing, utilities, etc.

Negotiation
Negotiation is a key skill to master to get the best deal when buying or selling something, or even getting the best salary and benefits when accepting a job offer. Most people do not like to negotiate, it is easier just to pay the asking price, or accept the amount offered from a buyer or employer. But if you become skilled at negotiation, you can end up with lots more dollars in your pocket instead of in the other guy's pocket.

Some skills that successful negotiators master include but not limited to the following:-
—*Willingness to walk*: Successful negotiators are willing to walk away if they can't get a good deal. Willingness to walk away gives you the confidence to ask for what you really want and drive a hard bargain. Often, you'll learn things in deals that

don't work out that help you get a better deal in the future.

—*Reasonable:* Good negotiators understand the market value of what they are negotiating and can understand the deal from the other party's perspective. If you seek an unreasonable deal, you are likely wasting everyone's time and won't end up with anything.

—*Perceptive:* They pick up clues from the other party to determine what kind of offer they would accept and use this information to negotiate the best deal possible.

Needs versus Wants
Separating needs from wants is a key personal finance skill. There is almost no limit to bigger, better, and newer stuff that you could decide to buy. The best way to make spending decisions is to become disciplined at distinguishing needs from wants. I like to think about the consequences of not buying something as a tool to distinguish needs from wants. For example, if I don't buy the new shoes I am considering, will I not be able to go to work? Will I miss events for my kids because I don't have any shoes that are acceptable to wear? Will I not be able to exercise safely? At some point new shoes can become a need, but if your old shoes are still doing everything you need your shoes to do, then new shoes are a want.

Lowering Interest Rates
A lot of people carry debt — the total credit card debt for Americans is set to hit $1 trillion dollars

this year. Of course, your best move is to pay off debt as quickly as possible to reduce your interest payments and to free up your money to invest or pursue other opportunities. But while you are paying off debt, it is worth putting in some effort to keep your interest rates as low as possible. The average credit card interest rate is nearly 15%. If you have credit card debt and don't keep an eye on the interest rate, you could easily end up paying 15% or more. Shopping around can almost always result in a better deal. If you have a good credit rating, you can likely find a balance transfer offer that will allow you to pay a balance transfer fee of about 3% and 0% interest for a year or more. I count maintaining favorable interest rates as a personal finance skill because you have to keep track of interest rates on your accounts and continuously find good deals on balance transfers. This skill can save you thousands of dollars per year on interest.

Continuous Investment
People who are financially successful do more than reduce spending and save money. They take the next step and invest money that they free up through smart spending decisions. This investment mentality is what allows the small amount of money you avoid spending to grow into real wealth that can change your lifestyle and allow you the freedom to pursue your interests. Regular saving over time adds up —even with small investment amounts. Continuous investment requires discipline to keep investing money for the future rather than spending it now. Savvy investors assess what kind of investments to buy and manage

their investment portfolio based on economic trends and the performance of their investments. The most important factor in being a successful investor is to make regular investments over the long term and let your wealth grow, my wife Dorothy does that very easily and successfully!

Window Shopping, Bargain and Deals Hunting
Frugal people are known for having good bargain hunting skills. Making a purchase is a challenge to find the way to spend the least amount of money to get what is needed. Bargain hunting usually involves using coupons and shopping around to find the best price. Sometimes buying a used item rather than a new item is the best bargain — you can save 50% or more buying used instead of new. Items such as tools or vehicles that are useful for years make good used purchases, but technology products often become obsolete so fast that buying new can be the best deal. Buying at the right time can be a key to finding bargains. I am always shocked at how cheap winter clothes and coats sell for in March at clearance sales. I bought most of my winter clothes for 90% off! My experience with electronic goods, buying them online by searching for better deals have proven to be the best way of getting better goods. Keep an eye out for bargains at store closing sales and clearance sales for items you know you will use later. An important part of bargain hunting is deciding on the best item to buy. If you can figure out the least expensive item that meets your needs, and then find the best price on that item, you are on your way to mastering bargain hunting skills.

Reuse

There is an old saying "Waste not, want not" that summarizes the personal finance skill of reuse well. If you don't waste anything, you will have plenty and not want for anything. Reusing things that most people would throw away is a key skill to save money and live well with less. When I was younger, I would always prefer to have new clothes rather than wear old clothes. Now I find comfort from the familiarity of wearing clothes with lots of memories attached to them. It seems like older stuff was constructed better than newer items, anyway. I think a lot of people are in the habit of throwing old things away just because they are old. Learn to keep reusing items until they no longer work, and then use them for something else. When my t-shirts start wearing out, I get sunburned through the holes in the fabric. Is it time to throw the shirt away? No! I use it for a rag.

Food Preparation

It is amazing how much restaurant food, fast food, and prepared food items from the grocery store people are buying these days. It does take some planning and work to prepare your own food at home, but you can save a ton of money and eat healthier, too. In addition to having basic cooking skills and equipment, having a plan is key to mastering the skill of preparing your own food at home. I know it works best at my house when we make a list of meals and then buy groceries with these meals in mind. Sometimes we even write on the calendar what is for dinner to avoid not coming up with something and ending up with expensive restaurant food.

Do It Yourself (DIY)
It seems like everyone that comes to my house to do something charges about $60 to $100 per hour. I try to minimize paying people to come over and try to take care of maintenance and repair myself instead to save money. I learned to do basic plumbing repairs and installation, including changing my car tire and basic electrical wiring and repairs around my home. Some people in my neighborhood have landscaping companies take care of mowing and weed control, but not me. The more things you can do for yourself, the more money you can save. Develop skills to do work for yourself instead of paying others to do it for you. You'll save money and get a great feeling of satisfaction when you can do the work yourself.

Saying No
Saying "no" is often the key to saving time and money. Would you like to subscribe to a magazine you don't want in order to help your neighbor's kid meet a fundraising goal? How about "no." Would you like to volunteer to drive 20 miles each way to participate in a committee meeting on your day off? Again, "no" works well here. There are times when you might want to contribute your time and money to a worthy cause, but there are many times you feel pressured into taking on something you don't really want to do. Learning to say "no" and not feel bad about it can save you a lot of time, money, and aggravation.

Efficiency
Efficiency is the skill of doing as much as possible with the least amount of resources. Efficiency can

mean making a single trip to do all of your shopping instead of taking multiple trips. Efficiency can mean driving a smaller vehicle that costs less and uses less fuel every day. Often, efficiency keeps paying back over time. For example, the efficient choice to live in a smaller house results in a lower mortgage payment and lower utility bills year after year. Energy savings is another example of efficiency in action. I spent a few hours and a few dollars to upgrade most of my light bulbs to LED. Due to this efficiency, I save money every month since lighting my house now costs almost nothing. Another form of efficiency is simply having less stuff. Do you really need eight different kinds of cleaning products under your kitchen sink? Having less stuff not only costs less, but less stuff takes less space as well. With fewer things around, it is easier to keep things organized and find what you need.

Contentment
I am sure that you can live with less, but can you be happy with less? Contentment is living with a positive attitude and being satisfied for all of the things you have instead of wishing that you had blingy stuff. I drive an 11-year-old car that runs well. It even has leather seats and all-wheel drive. What more do I need? People might not get a sense of status from the vehicle I drive, but I am clearly beyond worrying about that. Part of being content with what you have is to stop caring about what other people think. People who know me respect my work and my accomplishments, and I am not really concerned about what strangers think about my car. *Contentment means*

setting your own standard for happiness. This can be difficult to achieve as you look at the photos of expensive vacations, recreational vehicles, and new cars that your friends post on Facebook. It is hard not to want expensive stuff when it seems like everyone else is buying it. But the problem with pursuing happiness by buying expensive stuff is that there is always something else you'll need to buy in order to be happy. As soon as you get back from vacation, it is time to start thinking about where to go for the next one. After your new car isn't the newest on the block anymore, the excitement is gone. Buying happiness is like chasing a mirage. You can't really reach happiness through buying things, but you can spend a lot of money trying! Contentment is about finding happiness in the life you have right now, not the life you could have if only you had more money.

Financial Literacy

In past generations, cash was used for most daily purchases; today, it's rarely flashed – particularly not by younger shoppers. The way we shop has changed as well. Online shopping has become the top choice for many, creating ample opportunities to use and overextend credit – an all-too-easy way to accumulate debt, and fast. Meanwhile, credit card companies, banks and other financial institutions are inundating consumers with credit opportunities – the ability to apply for credit cards or pay off one card with another – and without the proper knowledge or checks and balances, it is easy to get into financial trouble.

Kristina Zucchi, CFA, a freelance financial writer, investor, and consultant who for over a decade, worked as an equity analyst for buy-side investment companies and in the private equity sector has observed that many consumers have had very little understanding of finances, how credit works and the potential impact on their financial well-being for many, many years. In fact, the lack of financial understanding has been signaled as one of the main reasons behind savings and investing problems faced by many not only in America but worldwide.

What Is Financial Literacy?

Financial literacy is the confluence of financial, credit and debt management and the knowledge that is necessary to make financially responsible decisions —decisions that are integral to our everyday lives. Financial literacy includes understanding how a checking (current) account works, what using a credit card really means, and how to avoid debt. In sum, financial literacy impacts the daily issues an average family makes when trying to balance a budget, buy a home, fund the children's education and ensure an income at retirement. A lack of financial literacy is not a problem only in emerging or developing economies. Consumers in developed or advanced economies also fail to demonstrate a strong grasp of financial principles in order to understand and negotiate the financial landscape, manage financial risks effectively and avoid financial pitfalls. Nations globally, from Korea to Australia to Germany, are faced with populations who do not understand financial basics.

The level of financial literacy varies according to education and income levels, but evidence shows that highly educated consumers with high incomes can be just as ignorant about financial issues as less-educated, lower-income consumers (though in general, the later do tend to be less financially literate). And it seems consumers are hesitant to learn. The Organization for Economic Co-operation and Development (OECD) cited a survey conducted in Canada that found that choosing the right investment for a retirement savings plan was more stressful than a visit to the dentist.

Trends

Compounding the problems associated with financial illiteracy, it appears financial decision-making is also getting more onerous for consumers. Five trends are converging that demonstrates the importance of making thoughtful and informed decisions about finances:

Consumers are shouldering more of the financial decisions: Retirement planning is one example of this shift. Past generations depended on pension plans to fund the bulk of their retirement lives. Pension funds, managed by professionals, put the financial burden on the companies or governments that sponsored them. Consumers were not involved with the decision-making, typically did not even contribute their own funds, and they were rarely made aware of the funding status or investments held by the pension. Today, pensions are more a rarity than the norm, especially for new workers. Instead, employees are being offered the ability to participate in 401(k) plans, in which they need to make investment decisions and decide how much to contribute.

Complex options: Consumers are also being asked to choose among various investment and savings products. These products are more sophisticated than in the past, asking consumers to choose among different options offering varying interest rates and maturities, decisions they are not adequately educated to make. Deciding on complex financial instruments with a large range of options can impact the consumer's ability to buy a home, finance an education or save for retirement, adding to the decision-making pressure.

Lack of government aid: A major source of retirement income for past generations was Social Security and Pension Funds. But the amount paid by Social Security is not enough, and it may not be available at all in the future. The Social Security Board of Trustees reported that by 2033 the USA Social Security trust fund may be depleted, a scary prospect for many. So now, Social Security acts more like a safety net that barely provides enough for basic survival.

Longer life spans: We are living longer. This means we need more money for retirement than prior generations did.

Changing environment: The financial landscape is very dynamic. Now a global marketplace, there are many more participants in the market and many more factors that can influence it. The quickly changing environment created by technological advances such as electronic trading make the financial markets swifter and more volatile. Taken together, these factors can cause conflicting views and difficultly in creating, implementing and following a financial roadmap.

Too many choices: Banks, credit unions, brokerage firms, insurance firms, credit card companies, mortgage companies, financial planners and other financial service companies are all vying for assets creating confusion for the consumer.

Why It Matters

Financial literacy is crucial to help consumers save enough to provide adequate income in retirement, while avoiding high levels of debt that might result in bankruptcy, defaults and foreclosures. A few years ago, a study from financial services company TIAA-CREF showed that those with high financial literacy plan for retirement and, in essence, have double the wealth of people who do not plan for retirement. Conversely, those with low financial literacy borrow more; have less wealth and end up paying unnecessary fees for financial products. In other words, those with lower financial literacy tend to buy on credit, and are unable to pay their full balance each month and end up spending more in interest. This group also does not invest, has trouble with debt and a poor understanding of the terms of their mortgages or loans. Even more worrisome, many consumers believe that they are far more financially literate than they really are.

And while this may seem like an individual problem, it is broader in nature and more influential on the entire population than previously believed. All one needs to do is look at the financial crisis of 2008 to see the financial impact on the entire economy that arose from a lack of understanding of mortgage products. Financial literacy is an issue with broad implications for economic health and an improvement can lead the way to a global economy that is competitive and strong.

The Bottom Line

Any improvement in financial literacy will have a profound impact on individuals and their ability to provide for their future. Recent trends are making it all the more imperative that people understand basic finances, because they are being asked to shoulder more of the burden of investment decisions in their retirement accounts – all while having to decipher more complex financial products and options. Learning how to read financially is not easy, but once mastered; it can ease life's burdens tremendously.

Personal Financial Tips

Dave Ramsey[iii] has personal financial tips for *young people before age 25*; the point is that the earlier you learn this stuff, the more success you'll have with money throughout your life. People older than 25 years can still benefit from these tips and they are universally applied.

Here are the tips:
- *Credit cards* will make you broke. Two words: stay away!

- *Car payments* aren't a way of life. You can pay for a nice used car with cash and avoid the average $500/month car payment.

- *Budgeting* is your best friend. It's simple: making a budget every month and sticking to it means you are going to win with money.

- *The Joneses* are broke. Don't try and keep up with the Joneses. They might look nice, but they're in debt up to their eyeballs and one emergency away from financial disaster.

- *It's okay to say no.* If a friend asks you to go on a trip or out to dinner, and you don't have the money, there's nothing wrong with saying no. Your friends will understand. And if they don't, you should find new friends!

- *Your parents* will eventually get old. That means you'll need to have "the conversation" with them about wills and estates before it's too late.

- You can be a *student without a loan.* Part-time jobs, scholarships, grants, more affordable schools—there are many ways to pay for college without debt.

- *Retirement* matters as much now as it does 30 years from now. Start saving for retirement as early as you can and put compound interest to work for you.

- *Wealth isn't evil.* A lot of people these days like to criticize rich people, but wealth isn't evil. The Bible never condemns money, only the *"love of money."*

- *Giving* is one of the best things you can do with money. The more you have, the more you can give away to bless others.

- The *tortoise beats the hare* every time. When it comes to money, patience will always pay off. Save and pay cash for stuff instead of using debt to "buy" them instantly.

- *Your first job* might not be your dream job. Learn, get experience, and build your career. The corner office might not come right away.

- *Your first house* might not be your dream house. Remember, your parents took 20 years to get their house. Don't expect that level of house right away.

- You should only get one *type of mortgage*: a *15-year,* fixed-rate. Your monthly payment should be no more than 25% of your take-home pay. Stay away from 30-year mortgages and ARMs no matter what!

- *Marriage* is much more difficult when you disagree with your spouse about money. Money fights are going to happen, but it's extremely important that you agree on the basics of money—like budgeting, no debt, and saving.

- *Be happy with what you have.* One word: contentment.

- You won't *get out of debt until you get mad.* To get out of debt, you've got to get sick and tired of being in debt. If you sorta, kinda want to get out of debt, you'll never make it.

- *Personal finance* is 80% behavior and only 20% head knowledge. It's all about behavior change. We all know if we're being irresponsible with money. But, many times, we go ahead and make bad choices anyway. That's got to change!

- *Get-rich-quick schemes* are good for one thing: making sure you get broke quick. There's no magic pill to get rich. It takes time and hard work.

- *Your parents* weren't perfect, but they probably knew more than you gave them credit for. The older you get, the smarter your parents get.

- *Never trust a payday lender.* Never. Payday lenders are the worst. The worst! They'll charge you 300% interest with a smile. Related: A Game You'll Never Win: The Payday Loan Trap

- *Don't travel the world* unless you can pay for it. And by "pay for it," I mean don't use credit!

- *It's okay to have stuff.* Just don't let your stuff have you. Don't mess up your priorities and let materialism get the best of you.

- *Your parents' house* is not a bed and breakfast. Move out! By the time you're 25, you should be long gone from your parents' house and out on your own. Sure, you might have transitional periods where you stay for a few weeks, but don't become a boomerang kid.

- *Eating out every night* is a really quick way to go broke. You can $10 yourself to the poorhouse if you aren't careful. The occasional night out is fine, but don't make it a habit, especially if you're already in debt.

If you're not yet wealthy but want to be someday, never purchase a home that requires a mortgage that is more than twice your household's total annual realized income.
— *Thomas J. Stanley*

Saving, Spending or Investing

Many new investors do not understand that saving money and investing money are *entirely different things*. They have different purposes, and play different roles, in your financial strategy and your balance sheet. Making sure you are clear on this fundamental concept before you begin your journey to building wealth and finding financial independence is vital because it can save you from a lot of heartache and stress. Cash deserves respect. The goal of cash is not always to generate a return for you. Perhaps the best place to start would be to spell out the differences between saving and investing for you, defining both concepts.

Saving money is the process of putting cold, hard cash aside and parking it in extremely safe, and liquid (meaning they can be sold or accessed in a very short amount of time, at most a few days) securities of accounts. Saving is setting aside money you don't spend now for emergencies or for a future purchase. It's money you want to be able to access quickly, with little or no risk, and with the least amount of taxes. Financial institutions offer a number of different savings options. This can include checking accounts and savings accounts secured by the governmental or federal agencies. This can include money market accounts (but not always money market funds as you need to look at the holdings and structure closely). Above all, cash reserves must be there when you reach for them; available to grab, take hold of, and deploy immediately with minimal delay no matter what is happening around you.

Many famous wealthy investors, as well as older investors who lived through the Great Depression, actually advocate keeping a lot of cash hidden on hand somewhere that only you know about even if it involves a major loss. It wasn't widely reported at the time but during the 2008-

2009 meltdown, some hedge fund managers were reportedly sending their spouses to get as much cash as they could out of ATMs because they believed the entire economy was going to collapse and there wouldn't be any access to greenbacks for a while. Only after capital preservation is accounted for do you worry about secondary considerations for money you have parked in savings; namely, keeping pace with inflation.

Investing money is the process of using your money, or capital, to buy an asset that you think has a good probability of generating a safe and acceptable rate of return over time, making you wealthier even if it means suffering volatility, perhaps even for years. Investing is buying assets such as stocks, bonds, mutual funds or real estate with the expectation that your investment will make money for you. Investments usually are selected to achieve long-term goals. Generally speaking, investments can be categorized as income investments or growth investments. True investments are backed by some sort of margin of safety, often in the form of assets or owner earnings. The best investments tend to be so-called productive assets such as stocks, bonds, and real estate.

In the book *The Millionaire Next Door*, author Thomas Stanley did an extensive analysis of the millionaires living in the United States. What he found might sound counterintuitive, but the majority of self-made millionaires aren't big spenders. In fact, they are the exact opposite. They live very modest, save money, buy used cars, and live within their means. Stanley concluded that these people are very conscious of how they spend their money. They will always look for ways for saving money and investing it.

Barack Obama

In many ways, the former President Barack Obama offers a great example to those burdened by debt. After graduating from Harvard Law in 1991, Obama and his wife Michelle held a combined total of $125,000 in student loan debt, but the President himself is now worth an estimated $11 million. Originating from a middle class background, he has achieved this success through hard work, patience and the cultivation of a responsible attitude toward spending and investing. When the President talked about personal finance, there was always an emphasis on the importance of retaining as much of your paycheck as possible. Back in 2011, during an inaugural White House conference for web-based finance journalists, Obama spoke eloquently about the need for fiscal discipline and a willingness to prioritize savings. More specifically, he touched on the relevance of understanding the fundamental differences between spending and investment and how this can have a positive impact in modern society.

How to Implement this Lesson

While there was some suggestion that the President was aiming a veiled barb at his Republican rivals, understanding the difference between spending and investment is an important step towards accumulating wealth. Although both require an initial outlay of money, an investment is something that delivers a tangible reward in the future, whether it is in the form of capital, equity or qualifications that can boost your earning potential. When you spend, however, you are purchasing goods and services that will not improve your quality of life or offer any type of long-term gain.

Purchases such as holidays, expensive dining experiences and evenings out belong to the latter category, as while they may be enjoyable, they offer no form of tangible asset return. There are also less fanciful examples of expenditure that come under the same classification, however, with big ticket items such as cars and personal computers being among the most prominent. Known as depreciating assets, these often functional and necessary products lose considerable value through extended use.

With this in mind, it is important to consider every purchase that you make as an individual and determine its potential to deliver a return. This way, it is possible to reduce the amount that you spend on luxury items and depreciating assets, before investing more of your capital into viable concerns. So the next time that you need to buy a car, for example, it is important to focus on high-quality, used vehicles that can be purchased affordably and have a less pronounced rate of depreciation.

The line between spending and investment is a fine one, especially when you consider how certain assets are likely to depreciate in value over time. As an individual, it is important to fully understand the difference between spending and investment, and apply this to every single purchase that you make. This will enable you to make the most of your disposable income, and commit as much money as possible towards improving your quality of life and accumulating long-term wealth.

How to Spend Wisely

Do you hate it when you really need money, but your wallet is empty? No matter how little or how much money you have, spending it wisely is a good idea; it enables you to get the most bang for your buck. Follow these tips to reduce expenditures in key areas and adopt a safer overall approach to shopping.

Create a budget. Track your spending and income to get an accurate picture of your financial situation. Save receipts or write down your purchases in a notebook as you make them.

Review your bills each month and add those expenses to your budget. Organize your purchases by category (food, clothing, entertainment, etc.). Categories with the highest monthly amounts (or monthly amounts you consider surprisingly high) may be good targets for saving money. Once you've tracked your purchases for a while, create a monthly (or weekly) limit for each category. Make sure the total budget is smaller than your income for that period, with enough left over for savings if possible.

Plan your purchases in advance. Making spur of the moment decisions can balloon your expenditures. Write down what you need to buy while you're calm and at home.

Make a preliminary trip before you go on your real

shopping trip. Note the prices of several alternatives at one or more stores. Return home without buying anything and decide which products to buy on your second, "real" expedition.[1] The more focused you are and the less time you spend in the store, the less you'll spend.

If you are motivated to treat each purchase as an important decision, you will make better decisions.

Do not accept free samples or try something on just for fun. Even if you don't plan on purchasing it, the experience can convince you to make a decision now instead of considering it carefully in advance.

Avoid impulse purchases. If planning your purchases in advance is a good idea, buying something on the spur of the moment is a terrible one. Follow these tips to avoid making shopping decisions for the wrong reasons:

- Don't browse store windows or shop for fun. If you're only buying something because you find the act of shopping fun, you'll likely end up spending too much on stuff you don't need.

- Don't make purchasing decisions when your judgment is impaired. Alcohol, other drugs, or sleep deprivation can harm your ability to make sensible decisions. Even shopping while hungry or listening to loud music can be a bad idea if you don't stick to your shopping list.

Retirement Preparations

Too often, people don't plan for retirement, and get a nasty wake-up call when life deals them an unpleasant surprise. Retirement planning is one of the issues that commonly lead people to consult financial advisers. One of its essential aspects is creating a plan to save and invest in order to provide a comfortable retirement income. Ideally, this starts many years ahead of retirement, even as early as your first paycheck. As retirement comes closer, planning for it expands to take in a host of other considerations, such as deciding when to retire, where to live and what kind of lifestyle you hope to have. When retirement becomes a reality, the focus shifts to carrying out the plan. The older we get, the more important this distinction between planning and preparing becomes. Too many life-changing things can happen without regard to our best-laid plans. Often they occur unexpectedly, resulting in emergency situations where urgent decisions have to be made. A stroke or a fall, a diagnosis of terminal illness, a broken hip that leaves someone unable to go back to independent living—and suddenly, right now, the family needs to find an assisted living facility, arrange for live-in help or sell a home.

Lulu Massawe, an advisor at *PFS Investment Inc.,* observed that one of the most overlooked subjects by the average person who earns an income is retirement planning. Most average people would like to live anyhow, spend money any which way and hope to be able to retire comfortably in the future. She argues that they even would want the government take good care of them some days after retirement. She compared that to farmers eating their own seed and awaiting a harvest at the end of the season. There are two major philosophies when it comes to the reality of retirement planning, one either plays now and pay later or pays now and play later. She stressed that one would be amazed at how a little bit of money savings goes a long way. That may sound vague, but consider this scenerio. If a person invested $500 a month into a good quality mutual fund from 1970 to 1990 allowed a client to begin withdrawing $5000 a month from 1990 until 2019 and left him or her with a portfolio worth $1.2 million that would still keep growing over time. He or she sacrificed only $500 a month and invested a total of $120,000 which in turn gave the access to over $2.5 million in retirement years. They paid the price earlier in order to play later. The question most of her clients would ask is where does one get that extra $500. Lulu advises them to either work an extra part time job, get tight on the budget or find a way. There are so many vehicles for retirement savings, which make available incredible tax benefits. You should not rest until you have explored them all.

A happy and fulfilling retirement means different things to different people. For you, it may mean transitioning from a full-time career into meaningful part-time work. Or perhaps you envision yourself spending more time with family, starting a garden or making regular visits to the golf course. Once you determine what will give you peace of mind in retirement, it's important to know how you can get there financially.

The following steps will help you get started with the plan.

Step 1: Define Your Retirement

You probably have some idea of how you'd like to spend retirement. Here's where you write your objectives down, listing the most important goals first. For now, don't focus on budget. Focus on ideas, and be as specific as you can. For example, instead of "travel," list "trips to the lake" or "walking tours of foreign countries." Instead of "stay involved in my community," write down "volunteer with kids one day a week."

Try to limit the list to your top five goals. Keep a scrapbook or start a journal depicting how you envision your retirement. Be practical: Your list should rule out unnecessary expenses. Make sure all your financial needs are met as you brainstorm. The more descriptive you are, the more tangible your retirement will be. This will help keep you focused on a realistic set of goals, which will make each of them more attainable.

If your goals are still general or vague, that's okay; too, you can simply start by outlining how you envision enjoying your retirement.

Step 2: Take Stock of Your 'Assets'

You know how much you bring home each month, how much you have in the bank and how much you have in your retirement account. But what about those other nontraditional assets that could help fund your retirement? Maybe you collect antiques or restore cars. Perhaps you're an accomplished pianist or have a half-written novel you want to finish. Many hobbies and skills can be turned into real income in your retirement years — trading antiques or teaching piano lessons, for example. Take the time to list all of your hobbies and skills. Don't worry if your list is small, but do list all of your passions and untraditional "assets". After that, start thinking about how you can morph those skills and hobbies into money-making endeavors.

Step 3: Evaluate Your Health — Now
To get the most out of your retirement —and life in general —you want to be as healthy as possible. And while few of us enjoy doctors' visits, a little preventive medical attention can go a long way. Schedule your checkups and preventive exams now, from an annual physical to teeth cleaning. At each appointment, work with your provider on a plan to improve or maintain your health. Commit (or recommit) to eating healthy, exercising and getting enough sleep. Healthy living doesn't have to be a chore. Many healthy foods are delicious and satisfying, and exercise can be fun (walk on the beach, anyone?). Commit to staying mentally sharp with brain games, puzzles and books. Staying in close contact with family and friends will help you maintain your health both physically and mentally and may aid in fighting off any blues that may arise once you are retired.

Step 4: Determine When to Collect Social Security
Hint: Later Is Better! Wouldn't it be nice if you saved and invested enough to enjoy financial freedom during retirement? Perhaps you did but for many that's not reality. Most of us will need the Social Security benefit we'll receive —both to pay for basic essentials and to support our retirement dreams. The age at which you choose to start collecting Social Security will have a direct impact on

how much you'll get in monthly benefits. The longer you wait to claim Social Security, the greater the benefit for you and your family.

Consider this: A widow or widower whose spouse claimed Social Security at full retirement age or older gets 100 percent of the benefits. A widow or widower whose spouse claimed benefits early gets 71 percent to 99 percent, depending on when the spouse began claiming. If you wait to claim, you'll also be eligible for delayed retirement credits, which give you an increase in benefits each year until you reach age 70. Whether you are married, single, widowed or divorced, it usually pays to wait to claim.

Step 5: Network Through Social Media
You need to build and maintain your network even in retirement. Use networking opportunities to showcase your talents. It's okay to brag about yourself to those who might help you fulfill your retirement dreams. Include a networking strategy in your retirement plan. It may involve spending an hour a day on Twitter or LinkedIn "conversing" with people who share your skills and interests, or starting a morning meet-up group at a local coffee shop to discuss ideas with other soon-to-be retirees. Such strategies will build relationships that in turn can grow your network. Also, be prepared to have clear, direct answers to such questions as "How can you use your talents and experience to contribute part time to an organization or cause?" The more socially active you are — online and offline — the more opportunities you are likely to create for yourself.

Step 6: Decide How Much You Want to Work
This is the classic cost-benefit equation: Unless you are financially set for life, you will have to either stretch limited money and give up some retirement dreams or stay in the workforce (in some capacity) to help pay for those dreams. As you write down your retirement goals, take into consideration how much work is necessary.

In the previous step, you were encouraged to look at your interests. But you should consider your lifestyle and preferences, too. "Work" will mean different things to different people in retirement. Either way, to ensure you successfully reach your goals, you'll have to decide how much time you want (or need) to spend at a job. Don't wait until after retirement to make the decision. Weigh right now the pros and cons of working — including how many hours per week. The sooner you get comfortable with this decision, the more secure you will be in your retirement planning.

Step 7: Create a Retirement Budget
Your budget needs to include:

- *How much money is coming in.*

- *How much it will cost to reach the goals you identified in step 1.*

- *How much debt you have.*

Start by tracking your income and expenses for a couple of months. Next, figure out how much money you'll need in retirement to support your chosen lifestyle. You'll also need to do a financial checkup of your investments. Make sure you are diversifying your money into multiple investments, investing in things you understand and won't cost you a ton in fees. If you are carrying debt, make sure your budget includes monthly payments to knock it down. Once you have a budget you know you can stick to, start putting it into action.

Step 8: Find New Ways to Cut Your Expenses
Your retirement may be right around the corner or years away. Regardless, saving more now will always make you better prepared. That doesn't mean all of your extra cash has to go into savings, but now is the time to find new way to cut your expenses. Start by listing your bills and then figure out ways to trim them. Maybe you don't need 100 cable channels or to eat out three nights a week. Even cutting one movie night a month can bring you closer to your retirement goals.

Got a green thumb? Growing your own vegetables can save you money that can be socked away for retirement. Don't ignore your debt as a way to save more. Cutting your debt now will mean less worry when you retire. One strategy that works for many people: Pay off your smallest debts first, regardless of interest rate. This gives you a sense of accomplishment and empowers you to go after the bigger debts, knowing you have the willpower to eliminate debt.

Step 9: Prepare for the Unexpected
Few of us head into retirement expecting the worst. But sometimes it happens. Prepare for the unexpected now and you won't get caught off guard later. Taking time to consider how you'd pay for — and respond to — everything from

minor issues like a roof leak to serious ones like a grave illness will help you weather those storms when they come. Discuss the big issues with your family or those closest to you. How much would it cost to make major repairs? What would you want to do (or what care would you want) if there was an illness in the family?

Step 10: Stick to Your Plan
This step may be challenging but it's definitely rewarding: sticking to your plan. We humans are creatures of habit and it's common to revert to old habits after trying a new course. There are ways of helping you avoid that such a join an online retirement community. These communities hold a wealth of information, ideas, tips, and for many is a source of comfort and strength.

Next, take stock of your protection. Do you have enough homeowner's insurance to cover a major calamity? Is your health insurance or long-term care insurance adequate? If your insurance coverage lacks some things, now is the time to increase it. Put money aside for the unexpected. Preparing now means you won't pay later.

Life Insurance
Life insurance can help reduce the financial impact on your loved ones in the event of your death. When you plan for life's uncertainties by having a life insurance policy, you provide your family the opportunity to help replace lost income, eliminate debt, pay for college, keep a business afloat, protect family wealth, or address other financial needs and goals while they adjust to a new life.

You work hard to make sure you can provide for your family's needs and goals. Preparing for your family's future, however, means more than investing appropriately for your goals and time horizon. For many people, it also involves purchasing the right amount of life insurance to protect their family's lifestyle.

A life insurance policy provides a payment in the event of your death that can help protect your family's lifestyle in the absence of your earning power. "Many people have financial goals they are trying to meet with hard-earned income—such as paying off a mortgage, putting a child through college, or supporting an elderly parent. Life insurance can help support your family goals" says Tom Ewanich[iv].

Why Life Insurance is a necessity

Pay Off Debts:
A life insurance policy can pay off any debts that you leave behind that would be a burden to your family. Debts such as a mortgage, credit cards, car loans and even your funeral expenses can have a dramatic impact on your family and their lifestyle.

Scott and Trish were happily married with two kids. Scott had a great job that he loved and was pulling down $150,000 a year. His employer provided two years' salary in life insurance, which Trish (who handled the finances) thought was sufficient until she talked to a friend of hers who was an insurance agent. Her agent friend warned her that any coverage through work is always a nice bonus, but it's never a good idea to rely on it. In the event that Scott were to quit, be fired or be laid off, his life insurance coverage would go away, leaving them completely exposed, and if 10 years had gone by, coverage would be much more expensive because Scott was now 10 years older. Most insurance experts recommend keeping your life insurance separate from any coverage offered by work. Consider work-related life insurance icing on your insurance cake. Trish took her friend's advice, and purchased a $750,000 term life insurance policy with a 25-year term. This coverage level would give her enough money to pay off their mortgage, put the kids through school and give her a bit of breathing room if the worst were to happen to Scott.

Provide for Your Kids:
A life insurance policy will ensure that your children can go to college, buy a home and even pay for their wedding if you die unexpectedly.
Peace of Mind: A term life insurance policy is an inexpensive way to give you and your family members peace of mind, knowing that they will be protected if something happens to you. You will no longer have to worry about their financial future and can rest easy knowing they will be able to continue their current lifestyle.

Kelly, a single mother, always thought it would be a good idea to buy life insurance to protect her children, but something always seemed to get in the way. Money was tight, or time was tight and she just never got around to it. Years later, Kelly purchased a small home; her daughter was then 18 years old and her son was 14. While she didn't exactly live paycheck to paycheck, her budget was pretty tight and didn't allow her much room for savings. One night while driving home from work, Kelly was struck head-on by a distracted driver. She died instantly. While Kelly's children were forced to deal with the tragic loss of their mother, they also had to face the fact that she left behind only a few thousand dollars in the bank and no life insurance, leaving them essentially broke after covering the cost of a very basic funeral. That is why life insurance is important.

Nobody knows what is coming around the corner. If you die unexpectedly, you can leave your spouse or children in a very tight spot. Term life insurance is extremely affordable. A 20-year policy with a death benefit of $500,000 for a healthy female can cost as little as $25 a month.

Funerals Are Pricey:
Even a basic funeral can cost $7,000-$10,000. A small life insurance policy will make sure your final expenses are covered so your family doesn't have one more worry at an already stressful time. Particular emphasis is put on immigrants that are still connected to their home countries. Transporting of bodies across borders can be very expensive and burdening to remaining family members and countrymen that have to deal with the logistics to transport the casket and body back to your home country. Unfortunately, many cultures feel like having last will and living will is a taboo and a bad omen.

George and Irene have been married for ten years, and for most of that time George has been lucky enough to stay home with the kids while Irene has been the primary breadwinner. While Irene earns a good living, she would struggle to cover the cost of a nanny or other childcare provider if something were to happen to George. George provides a variety of services to the family. He takes care of childcare, transportation, managing the household and their finances. He also deals with repairs and maintenance for their home. George also earns a small income doing handyman services around the neighborhood. They decide that in the event something happened to George, a life insurance policy would ensure that Stacy would have enough money to hire the necessary help or take a few years off to stay at home as the family learns to cope with the loss. Stacy purchases a 20-year term policy with a death benefit of $750,000 that will give her the financial means to replace the services George provided for the family as well as cover the cost of sending the kids to college.

Supplement Your Retirement
Permanent life insurance policies accumulate a cash value over the life of the policy that can be borrowed against tax-free. These policies can be used to supplement your retirement if your other investments fall short. These policies often come with fairly high fees, so be sure to compare the costs to those of other investment vehicles.

Protect Your Business:
Regardless of whether you are using a life insurance policy to insure a key employee, fund a buy/sell agreement or simply provide a tax-free cash infusion (borrowing against the cash value of a permanent policy), life insurance can be a major asset to your business.

John's board of directors was concerned

that if something happened to John, the company would suffer a tremendous financial loss. The board felt that a key man insurance policy was needed. A key employee life insurance policy is put in place to protect a business from losses if an invaluable employee dies. The company decided to take out a very large life insurance policy on John, over his strenuous protests. John felt that he was in fine shape and would live to a ripe old age. Unfortunately, John was wrong. He suffered a major heart attack and died a few years after the policy went into effect. Sales and the stock price immediately plummeted after his death, and the death benefit from the life insurance policy kept the company afloat for the next 12 months while the new CEO rebuilt investor trust and got the company back on track.

Marina Theodotou, EdD is an entrepreneur and an economist (BA Honors, MA) with a Six Sigma Black Belt (Bank of America 2003) currently based in Nicosia, Cyprus.

[ii] Dr. Penny Pincher "12 Personal Finance Skills Everyone Should Master" https://www.wisebread.com/12-personal-finance-skills-everyone-should-master

[iii] Dave Ramsey, Financial Adviser and Radio Host https://www.daveramsey.com/blog/25-things-to-know-before-you-turn-25

[iv] Tom Ewanich, a vice president and actuary at Fidelity Investments Life Insurance Company.

six

Newcomers to Wealth

By three methods we may learn wisdom: First, by reflection, which is noblest; second, by imitation, which is easiest; and third by experience, which is the bitterest.

—*Confucius*

I heard an old story of the couple in the west coast of United States that decided to sell their house and all the belongings they had in order to go around the world to look for gold that they could involve in that business. After few years of hopping in different places and countries seeking for gold to no avail, they decided to return to their home place in the west coast. To their surprise they found their former house fenced together with other houses in their former neighborhood and armed security protecting the area. When they asked what is going on and why tight security in the area; they were told that the company recently found gold mine underneath those houses and owners were given an option to be compensated or own shares in the gold mine! So the main lesson is "*explore your options thoroughly before leaving to other places looking for opportunities*". Before we venture into new territory, we should make sure we exhaustively explore our options locally. I have learned that most places have ample opportunities but the problem is we do not have the eye to see and seize them. I lived in Southern African country of Botswana for about five years in the Kalahari Desert working with the San communities. The desert is harsh and very little or no rain for most part of the year and business opportunities in this environment needed high level of creativity. Tourists from around the world would come to the Kalahari Game Reserves and also visit villages around to explore indigenous culture and ways of life. The most abundant resource they have is *desert sand*! Well packaged and labeled that quickly turned to be a commodity that tourist will buy as a souvenir to take back home to remind them or show other their experience in the desert. Other places, such as Cape Town, South Africa at the Cape Point, this is near the lowest habitable point on the southern hemisphere where Atlantic and Indian oceans meet; tourist literally buy ocean water as souvenir, again an abundant resource that is found locally.

> *There are plenty of business opportunities around us, what we need is a creative entrepreneurial discernment to be able to discover, recognize and guts to seize them.*

Newcomers to Wealth

The psychologist and author James Grubman[i] says that families new to wealth face different challenges than those with "old money"; the challenges are similar to those confronting immigrants to a new land. We have all heard the phrase — Rugs to riches refers to any situation in which a person rises from poverty to wealth and in some cases from absolute obscurity to heights of fame, fortune and celebrity—sometimes instantly.

"Immigrants to wealth" is the phrase Grubman uses to describe first generation millionaires. The parents have grown up in the lower or middle class —struggling to establish themselves and succeed while the children now live in the new world of riches and wealth, where the rules are different and can be baffling. One of Grubman's main points is that immigrants to the new world of wealth should consider their "capital" as not just their financial wealth but to look beyond their financial capital to the life resources and values they have to safeguard and develop. In order to avoid squandering wealth after just a few generations, focus has to be on all aspects of family capital. The four different types of capital are namely financial, intellectual, social, and human, abbreviated as FISH, after the work of wealth psychologist Lee Hausner[ii].For many families new to wealth, human capital is the hardest to develop inter-generationally. It has to do with instilling core values focused on education, achievement, leadership, duty and obligation. Without money to act as incentive, parents have to work wisely and diligently to combat complacency and a sense of entitlement.

When kids ask for something perhaps a bit too extravagant, the adults need to be able to say, "No, we won't." Kids like to test limits and push buttons. As parents some of us know this first-hand: It's important to learn how to say no, in no uncertain terms: "Sure, we can buy that for you, but we choose not to. It's not consistent with our values."Of course, this is easier said than done. It requires that families know how to articulate their values and know how to make these values real for their kids. All this is hard to do in any family, but especially those new to wealth.

> *How can I make sure that my children grow up to be economically productive adults? Most millionaire next door types were raised by parents who were disciplined and frugal. Parents in such cases typically ran their households like a well run, efficient business. More often than not their children adopted a similar economic lifestyle.*
> —*Thomas J. Stanley*

Greener Pastures Syndrome

How many times have we heard the cliché, *"The grass is always greener on the other side?"* While the overuse of this phrase has mostly dulled its impact, people who experience the "grass is greener syndrome" endure a significant struggle with commitment. The hallmark of the *"grass is greener syndrome"* is the idea that there is always something better that we are missing. So rather than experiencing stability, security, and satisfaction in the present environment, the feeling is there is more and better elsewhere, and anything less than ideal won't do. Whether it's with relationships, business, careers, or where you live, there is always one foot out the door.

The problem with this is the greener grass is usually based on fantasy and fear. The fear comes from several possibilities, including fear of being trapped in commitment, fear of boredom, fear of loss of individuality, and fear of daring something big or valuable. Along with these fears comes the issue of compromise. In people who fear commitment, comprising certain desires, needs, and values for the sake of the unity can feel like oppressive sacrifice. When this happens, the perception is that there is something else out there that will allow us to have all that we crave, want, and value, and that it will happen on our terms. This is where the element of *fantasy* comes in, and with the fantasy comes projection. We're going to want what we don't have, and there's a fantasy that we'll get what we don't have, and that the parts that we're currently happy with won't be sacrificed in this change. However, what ends up happening is that after the *"honeymoon phase"* of making the change, we find ourselves wanting to flip to the other side of the fence again because we discover that there are other things that we don't have, and because the novelty of the change wears off. It ends up being true, that we always want what we don't have, even if we've already jumped the fence several times.

This is where projection comes in, when the grass is greener on the other side, we're usually (if not always) placing personal unhappiness with ourselves onto something outside of us — generally a partner, career, living environment, etc. We rely on polishing our external environment to soothe a deeper internal dissatisfaction. Though the environment changes when jumping the fence, after a brief internal high, without constant stimulation and newness, the dissatisfaction becomes the same. *I think the cliché should be changed to this: "The grass is only as green as we keep it."* The grass always starts out a nice and shiny green ('honeymoon phase'), but will begin to wear a bit with use. Then, it still needs to be maintained in order to stay a nice shade of green. The dulled green (or even brown) grass on our current side of the fence would be greener if we nurture it. The shiny green grass on the other side of the fence is our wish for our internal selves — to be happy, unscathed, and fully satisfied. The truth is, as human beings, we are all in some ways less than perfect, and therefore, the shiny grass is an illusion. Our job is to keep the grass as green as possible, which may take some outside help. But no matter what, it won't remain as green as the moment we first set foot on it. There are certainly times where another situation is a better situation than the current one (for example, a healthy relationship versus an abusive one; a job that's more fulfilling to you versus an unfulfilling job).

But the "grass is greener syndrome" has its own particular presentation, primarily rooted in following patterns:-

- *Repetition:* A pattern in your life of constantly wanting better and repeatedly seeking change in relationships, jobs and environment. Tendency of hip hopping from one relationship, job or situation to the other.

- *Perfection:* It is one thing to go from an abusive relationship to a positively-functioning relationship, but it's another to feel that a string of functioning relationships are never good enough. There may be a search for the fantasized ideal taking place.

- *Wanting to have and eat your cake:* This is in line with the struggle of compromise. If you must have every want and perceived need that stimulates you, then it's likely that the grass will never be green enough unless you're the only one on the grass — and even then, it won't be green enough because of what may be missing from this picture.

- *Wanting to run away:* If you see a pattern of being unable to settle in one geographic place, relationship, business, job, etc., there are deeper reasons for this than just not being in the "right" environment. We refer it as the *vagabond spirit* based on the ancient Jewish story of young man "Cain" who killed his brother "Abel"; the murderer was haunted by the death of his brother and wandered the earth as the punishment from God.

- *Ultimate dissatisfaction:* If you enjoy constant change, and living out this sort of life, then there's technically nothing wrong with this. But if the reason for the constant change comes from repetition of dissatisfaction, and if you're looking to become more secure, stable and settled, then this is an issue to look into.

The best way to deal with the *"grass is*

greener syndrome" is to learn the underlying reasons beyond the abstract ideas of idealizations, perfectionism, and the inability to commit. Learn how to nurture and increase connection to what's current so the relationships are maintained and strengthened rather than become unsatisfying. The idea is to build an internal place of stability, rather than jumping around in your external life to compensate for a lack of internal stability.

Economic Refugees

Many Western countries have experienced massive migrations of skilled and non-skilled individuals primarily as economic refugees seeking safe havens for their families and better quality of life. I personally happen to have firsthand experience of migrating from my native country to other countries. Most of my life I have been called a foreigner or an alien and other places have more derogative names to refer to aliens in their communities. Many times immigrants in pursuit of better life travel for many days and exhaust most of their savings, and barely speak the language. The irony is most of them after very short period of time become extremely successful compared to natives who have all the advantages and privileges of the system. In attempt to answer the paradox there are some few observations that are worth noting about immigrants particularly those going to western world.

Love is overrated: Immigrants don't go to other countries to do what *they love*; they go there *to generate wealth*. Happiness is the last thing on their minds because all they care about is making money and achieving their goals. With that money they can provide a better future for their families and, most importantly, provide their kids with the things that they themselves never had when growing up. Most of the immigrants still support extended families and friends in their countries of origin and other bigger causes of their passion. The big difference between immigrants and natives is that, most of the natives were taught to do what they love. For example, in the first world if you want to be an astronaut, throughout your life your parents and teachers encouraged you to *follow your dreams.* Immigrants, however, are taught to do whatever makes money, helps earn a living and to pursue their dreams later when it is conducive.

The 80-hour workweek: Do you love the 4-hour workweek? Well, immigrants don't! If they don't believe in the 40-hour workweek, there is no way they believe in the 4-hour workweek. Instead of trying to figure out how they can work fewer hours each week, they try to figure out how they can work more hours. Sixty, seventy, and even eighty hours are the number of hours immigrants try to work each week.

My wife and I came to America about twenty years ago, early in our life we both had two full time jobs, which means we were literally working eighty hours every week. And although working eighty hours a week doesn't give you the best quality of life, it gives you the potential to make more money and compensate for years that you were not in the labor market.

Pick and Choose: Immigrants do not cherry pick jobs based on the conditions or salary. They are conditioned to work hard and pick any job that is available to them. Most immigrants do not quit before getting another better paying job and their only motivation is to get paid and make money in order to achieve their dreams. While natives complain and whine about the working conditions, their counterparts are grateful for the opportunity the workplace provides and look at the same conditions using a totally different lens. Employers and investors love the immigrants because of their work ethics, if given a small stake in the business, they'll work a lot harder than if you paid them to work eighty hours per week.

Immigrants stick together: One thing that I never forgot is that when I immigrated to Southern African country called Botswana, I was provided accommodation by a Church pastor, Ms Theresia who was also an immigrant, we barely knew each other only met once or twice back in our home country. She helped me navigate the new environment and connected me to other immigrants in a different region that happened to be former colleagues from university; Humphrey, Wilson and Kenneth, and again we barely knew each other except going to the same college.

My epiphany came about after meeting Otha Archie, former UN worker who retired and settled in Botswana as a business woman and immigrant from Barbados. She freely mentored and helped me open my own veterinary practice and made available her own commercial facility and a truck for me to get started on my feet. When

Dorothy and I migrated to USA, our daughter Emmy was only 2 years old; Lucas my brother in-law (also an immigrant) helped us out navigate our new life in North Carolina. He was very instrumental from providing free temporary living accommodation to helping us find a job. Immigrants help each other succeed in many aspects and stick together as a family. Even after being in the US for over twenty years, we still buy some used stuff from Thrift stores to used cars and we encourage our children to think that way as there's nothing wrong being frugal. It's easier to save money than it is to earn it especially if you are working 80-hour weeks. Immigrants are never afraid to ask for discounts because they know that if you never ask, you'll never receive. From bargaining at stores and markets to only buying things that are on sale, immigrants always find ways to save money and quickly climb to the top.

Education is everything: When times get tough, the one thing that increases the odds of success is having a good education. Whether it is a teenage or a middle-aged immigrant, it is never too late to go back to school. They value education so much that they are ready to sacrifice anything to earn it.

My wife changed professions from being a certified accountant from our native country to starting all afresh in the different field of nursing. She climbed through all ranks of educational credentials from a patient sitter, certified nurse assistant, through practical licensed nurse, registered nurse to doctoral degree in nursing practice (DNP) while having a full time job, a mother of three young children and a committed wife.

Studies show that if you have a bachelor's degree, on average you'll make $900,000 more over your lifetime than someone who just has a high school diploma. And if you have a master's degree, you'll make $1,200,000 more in your lifetime than a high school graduate[iii]. There is no excuse for not going to college as there are online and nighttime classes that can serve as convenient alternative for traditional schooling that may interfere with job schedule and family responsibilities.

They never take "no" for an answer: Just because someone tells you no; it doesn't mean that you can't change that *"no"* to a *"yes"*. When I first immigrated to the US, I could not find a job as a veterinary doctor, which is my primary occupation. So, when I was told no by one particular veterinary hospital, I moved on to another, until I finished them all in the city that I live about fifteen pet and animal hospitals. I remember telling one of the pet hospital owners that I would work for free if he would only give me an opportunity to do so.

Months later, he decided to hire me and, more importantly, the owner was so impressed with my service and agreed to sponsor me for my eligibility to US permanent residence or commonly known as *green card*. If someone tells you no, it just means not right now but could turn into a yes later on.

Comparative Analysis: Although they may not be

living in a fancy home or a rich neighborhood when they first immigrate over, those living conditions are still better than the ones they came from. This is why they rarely complain about life because there really is nothing to be sad about. In their eyes, life is truly good. They have a roof over their heads, and their kids are getting a great education. They approach life from a totally different angle and view it using a comparative lens. They are used to make things happen from nothing, or very limited resources and find it easier when surrounded by diverse resources especially in the west were literally everything is available.

Next time you encounter immigrants, don't judge them base of the job they have, the way they talk with a funny accent, or the clothes they wear. Be careful as some of the richest immigrants I know still drive their old beat-up cars and buy their clothes from Wal-Mart and only when they are on sale. Immigrants are successful because of *their beliefs* and the way they *were brought up*. So, take a page out of their book and learn a few things because it isn't too late for you to pick up a few useful approaches to life and, more importantly, become successful.

Red Bull

What's this Red Bull guy story with Dietrich Mateschitz, some strange last name? The founder of Red Bull has an interesting story on how the business leverage to where it is right now. He apparently went to Thailand where they're making a drinkcalled *Krating Daeng* which in the native language means *red bull*. He asks, "My gosh! What is this drink made for?" They told him, "For truck drivers so they don't fall asleep when on steering wheel." After taking few sips of the drink he liked it and brought it to America. He started selling it and puts Red Bull on it and now he's worth $15.7 billion on a drink called Red Bull. You know how many billions of Red Bulls you have to sell to have a net worth of $15.7 billion? That's how many he sold so far. What has happened is he got globally connected. Immigrants are connected to other places and constantly in another country. They are not worried about going to another country because you're already used to it and being strangers. Statistics show that 40% of Fortune 500 CEOs are immigrants or the child of an immigrant that started the company. Furthermore, over 10% of Forbes 400 richest men in America are immigrants. Elon Musk the founder and owner of Telsa Motors is one of them and Google cofounder and Alphabet president Sergey Brin leads the pack as the wealthiest immigrant billionaire, with a $37.5 billion fortune.

Foundations to Success

Develop yourself

It is necessary to prove what and how things work then systematically grow and expand your territory. Many are times that we are tempted to work harder on our work, business and what it is required of us and tend to forget to work on ourselves to develop what it takes to become who we are supposed to be. Adding value on ourselves is the fundamental step towards valuable contribution to the marketplace. A better you harnesses the delivery of the better service you are envisioning to your customers, clients or people you intend to reach. A genuine smile and interest on people goes further than an artificial and fake smile just to entice customers to buy. People know when they are enticed by fake personalities and attributes, at the end of the day if the emphasis is only on the outward expression and not inner transformation work becomes mechanical, tedious, uninteresting and dull. Work hard on inner transformation and outward expression becomes natural and second nature. There is nothing wrong with being ambitious and looking forward to expanding territories. However, clarity and a good handle of how things work in terms of processes and systems proves to be instrumental in the process of replicating success from one location to the other.

My wife and I decided to open multiple locations for the business we are running and we went ahead and increased six more sites in different cities. We had not prepared and studied what it takes to replicate the successes we have locally to other sites. We overlooked most of the fundamentals things like training, supervision, planning, regular meetings for communication flow, delegation and dynamics of different environment from what we are used to. All of a sudden the business became overwhelmingly burdening, we did not realize the revenue and profits as we projected. Moreover, we lost the time we used to enjoy with each other and everything we set in the satellite office collapsed and we had to close and sell all the licenses we had to operate in those areas. What does it take to replicate success then? Careful analysis of the present recipe of systems, processes and dynamic interactions of all the factors patiently studied together with putting aside the ego resulting from small local success. It takes a character to admit that you still need to learn and consider how things work because what works here might not work there!

Start small
This is my favorite advise to everyone I meet and ambitious to start a new endeavor, first thing I emphasize is start small with baby steps but maintain a big vision with global outlook. Operate locally but do not close doors for cross border opportunities. The key thing here is to *get started* because many people have great dreams and big ideas and grandiose goals to be achieved but never have the guts to get started. They lack the confidence, skill and initiative to get started; either overwhelmed by the vastness of their own idea and dream or sometimes it's just mere procrastination. The tragedy for most dreamers and visioneers is the fact that they get overwhelmed by their own idea and do not know how to start. They get mental paralysis since their mind fails comprehend where and how to get started.

I personally experienced this state for 2 years since I got an idea to establish a university that will serve the local and international community. *The secret was to take the big dream and chunk it down to small pieces that are manageable and sizeable to implement.* We had to take the entire idea of establishing a university and size it down to pieces that can be quickly established and implemented. Small steps and work them out on the timeframe while focusing on the bigger picture. We started by establishing and registering an institute that slowly and systematically grew until it eventually became a university.

Important projects carrying big dreams and ideas take time. *"Rome wasn't built in a day"*— French proverb in the late 1100s;is an injunction or plea for people to be patient and systematic on their constructive ideas that have to make a difference in the society.

Procrastination is the act of delaying or postponing a task or set of tasks. Human beings have been procrastinating for centuries. The problem is so timeless, in fact, the ancient Greek philosophers like Socrates and Aristotle developed a word to describe this type of behavior; *Akrasia*. Akrasia is the state of acting against your better judgment. It is when you do one thing even though you know you should do something else. Loosely translated, you could say that *akrasia* is procrastination or a lack of self-control.

So, it is the force that prevents you from following through on what you set out to do. In order to hone this strategy to overcome Akrasia is by making tasks more achievable as you break them down, we will consider the remarkable productivity of the famous writer Anthony Trollope[iv]. He published 47 novels, 18 works of non-fiction, 12 short stories, 2 plays, and an assortment of articles and letters. How did he do it? Instead of measuring his progress based on the completion of chapters or books,

Trollope measured his progress in 15-minute increments. He set a goal of 250 words every 15 minutes and he continued this pattern for three hours each day. This approach allowed him to enjoy feelings of satisfaction and accomplishment every 15 minutes while continuing to work on the large task of writing a book. Making your tasks more achievable is important for two reasons. First, small measures of progress help to maintain momentum over the long-run, which means you're more likely to finish large tasks. Secondly, the faster you complete a productive task, the more quickly your day develops an attitude of productivity and effectiveness. I have found this second point, the speed with which you complete your first task of the day, to be of particular importance for overcoming procrastination and maintaining a high productive output day after day.

Associate with achievers
People who have track record of successful ventures will always influence you to also become successful if you allow them. As the saying goes, success leaves tracks and it is transferable. People who have similar interests, ideas, or characteristics tend to seek out and associate with one another hence the old English saying —birds of the same feathers flock together. Most beneficial disciplines and behaviors that make people successful are generally applicable in many fields and walks of life. I personally use to wonder why would we listen to celebrities even in things that are not associated with the areas we celebrate their achievements. I came to realize that because of their massive success in one area, somehow they have already figured out the secret, recipe and necessary disciplines applicable to become successful, and guess what—people listen to them

(even if sometimes giving wrong information) because it is known that these skills are transferable to other aspects of life that we are striving for mastery.

The facts below demonstrate the power of association in our lives:-

- *Association is vital to every man in pursuit and fulfillment of destiny*

- *Who you follow determines what follows you.*

- *Where you stand determines how and what you view.*

- *You company determines your accomplishment.*

- *Your location determined your allocation.*

- *Your position determines your possession.*

- *Your posture determines your posterity.*

- *The direction you face determines the attraction you make.*

- *Your association determines your influence.*

Albert E.N.Gray spent a lifetime trying to discover the common denominator of success. He concluded that the successful person has formed the habit of doing things that failures don't like to do. Successful people don't like doing them either. But their dislike is subordinated to the strength of their purpose. Nobody likes to give pain to the muscles in the gym. Yet successful people subordinate the pain to the higher purpose of being healthy. Let's subordinate our dislikes to a strong purpose. We may not enjoy every task on the path towards the goal. But success is about doing things that make us uncomfortable[v].

Catapult Effect

As a kid growing in East Africa, we did not have readymade toys that most kids these days enjoy. We learned to make our own toys and one was a *catapult*, this is a device that accumulates tension and it suddenly releases an object to hurl it some distance away. We used it to hit different sport targets and also in those days to hunt for sport. The catapult will have three main components; the Y-shaped handle which we will make from the branch of a tree with that shape, the rubber bands and the leather pad which holds the object to be released.

When I was considering opening college campuses to different countries, a good friend and a mentor asked me—"Lucas, have you considered a catapult effect?"; Since he also grew in the same environment like me in East Africa, it was easy for me to slow down and consider the catapult and how it applies to the business expansion. The Y-shaded handle serves as an anchor point of pivot. All the tension collected in the rubber bands depends on how firm the handle is held and could withstand the pull. The handle is your pivot point where all the tension, pull and power comes from and it has to be strong and stable. I realized that by that time we were not yet strong and stable enough to be able to withstand supporting expansions overseas though they looked very lucrative. The stronger the handle (or the headquarters for this matter) the further the object can be released to hit the target (remote sites).

> *Sink deep your roots and develop strong muscles before you start operating beyond borders.*

Many beginner entrepreneurs become overly and unrealistic ambitious and want to operate beyond borders before taking time to learn the challenges and what it takes to expand overseas.

Few important things to look carefully when considering to operate across borders or to have multiple sites include:-

Capital: This normally can be liquid money that can be used to acquire real estate if the operation needs one, paying of salaries, training of new staff to understand the business model and other expenses that are essential to get you started in the new site. If not carefully considered, it might mean that you might be stuck before you even start. It took us 6 months of paying salaries, furnished and pay rent in the commercial facility that we converted into an institute before we were allowed to start advertizing and recruiting students! So, it is always important to consider all the nuances that are particular to what you do.

Culture: Consideration of cultural and sociological aspects and differences, attitude towards foreign goods and services is very important to expansion of your territory. Culture is the social behavior and norms found in human societies and it is basically how people live, their belief system and everyday life in terms of what is acceptable or not. It will be unwise to expand a mortuary business in the society that believes strongly that bodies ought to be buried the same day. In parts of the world where there is a strong bond and moral belief that families ought to take care of their elderly by living with them until they die; it won't be easy to introduce services that deal with assisted living or retirement homes for the elderly. I personally visited a country in Africa where people strongly believe that anything sold on the website is a scam! They would rather see it physically before buying it by cash or mobile money or there should be a mobile application (app) to sell that item but not a website; as many people have lost money on scam websites and now it has become a taboo. To expand your business to this society most energy has to be channeled to overcome that taboo for it to be successful.

Some other places believe strongly that goods from particular countries are of superior quality compared to other countries. Even if in the reality these goods are of the same quality. So long as goods have a tag "Made in Country X" it will sell regardless of the quality because of preconceived notion that Country X makes superior products. If you are from Country Y and there is a negative preconception about goods from your area, you will need a different strategy to penetrate the market in order to go against the norm. Researching and studying belief systems and society norms that directly affect your business enterprise is very important for the sustained success.

Local Regulations: This is an aspect that we overlook and presume that whatever regulations we have in our locality applies universally. For example, in USA it takes few minutes to register a company using online services, same day you can apply by telephone to get the tax number and also local county license to operate a simple business. In some states they have removed the requirement for county license. So within few minutes you can start a business and be fully and legally operational. While in other places of the world there is too much bureaucratic red tape and hoops one has to go through to start a business, it may even take six months to a year before you can operate legally. It took me at least three weeks to open a bank account in one particular country that we were considering to invest. All that time we had to endure the risk of having lots of cash in the hotel room we stayed and sometimes walking around with it. It reminded me of the difference we had from other places that banks took few minutes to open an account and secure your money. It can be as simple as opening a bank account or as complex as acquiring business licenses and all legal documents to allow you to operate a simple business, the rule of the thumb is to consider the local regulations before you launch.

Environment: This covers a big landscape from the availability of raw material locally, internet connectivity, transport, roads and means of telecommunication. Thorough assessment and consideration of these factors will always determine the success level. I recently visited a country in the Caribbean islands where internet connectivity was so scarce that people had to buy data cards which give access to internet on an hourly basis and only few places in the city will have hotspots for accessibility. In this island most of the transactions were done by cash and internet usage was not that much compared to other places in the same region. Considering establishing an online shop in this region would not be wise because the environment does not support cheap and simple usage of internet connection to a common person. Likewise, in big cities there is a trend of one stop shopping centers where consumers purchase everything from one shop or shopping complex for convenient purposes. Expanding a small family owned shop to one of these big cities needs careful consideration in terms of where the shop needs to be located and the consumer behavior. Big cities especially in the western world are hectic and fast paced compared to small cities in the rural areas where life is slow paced and very personal.

Market: Everything in the world of business depends on market; otherwise you will remain with stockpiles of unsold goods or unneeded services. Careful exploration and assessment of market preferences, prejudice, purchasing power, and current competitions is essential to successful launching on the remote site. Investigate industry trends on the goods and services that you are envisioning to offer and try to quantify the total market for your product or service. It is paramount that you know who your target market is and how do they behave. Together with that as you are investigating the market; also investigate your competition both local and national, —what is it that you are offering and how does it compare with the competition?

Look into overall strategy for selling your products or services and clearly establish a pricing policy that is reflective of your market preference and purchasing power. What sort of after sales or customer service policy will you put in place in order to distinguish yourself from others and serve your customers better? Lastly, invest time in developing a formal marketing plan that will become your roadmap to scaling your business to other places.

[i] James Grubman "Strangers in Paradise: How Families Adapt to Wealth Across Generations" 220 pages,

[ii] Lee Hauser "The Legacy Family: The Definitive Guide to Creating a Successful Multigenerational Family" 2016

[iii] Tamborini, Christopher R., Chang Hwan Kim, and Arthur Sakamoto. 2015. "Education and Lifetime Earnings in the United States." Demography 52: 1383–1407.

[iv] Anthony Trollope (24 April 1815 – 6 December 1882) was an English novelist of the Victorian era https://en.wikipedia.org/wiki/Anthony_Trollope

[v] Brian Tracy, Million Dollar Habits: Practical, Proven, Power Practices to Double and Triple Your Income Copyright ©2004 by Entrepreneur Media Inc. ISBN 1-932156-70-4

seven

Fake Rich People

"One person pretends to be rich, yet has nothing; another pretends to be poor, yet has great wealth"

—King Solomon

F ake it till you make it— is an English apho-
rism which suggests that by imitating confidence, competence, and an optimistic
mindset, a person can realize those qualities in their
real life. But there's a fine line between that senti-
ment and a flat-out lie and you had better be on the
right side of it if your life or career is at stake. Many
of us would like to improve some element of our
character or personality that we feel might be holding us back. Perhaps be more confident, disciplined
or ambitious. If we can clearly identify what that is,
we can start by changing our behavior with the goal
of having it become more natural over time. Behav-
ing like the person you want to become is about
changing the way you feel and the way you think.

Imitating the Lifestyle of the Wealthy

Spotting a wealthy man or woman can be difficult
and not straightforward as we normally would
think. There is a lot misconception about how

they look, behave and carry themselves as wealthy. If you have never read the book "The Millionaire Next Door" by Thomas J. Stanley, taken a class on investments or read an article about money. Assuming you know nothing about personal finance the first things that come to your mind thinking of someone who is "rich" are images of expensive suits, fancy cars, or lavish mansions. Unfortunately, that is not what "rich" means; society has programmed our brains to believe that is what means to be wealthy. We conjure up images like this when imagining productive and successful people. As a society, we all have a ton of work to do in debunking the common perceptions of "rich people". Until then, here are a few observations I have about the fake rich:

Characteristics of the fake rich

Here are a few things you may notice about people who I would consider to be "fake rich":

Good salaries: Fake rich people need to make good money to keep up their materialistic lifestyle. The fake wealthy people usually have more than average salary, sometimes six figures and very steady jobs that make them good money, however, they are always broke and that money seems not to be enough to maintain their lifestyle.

Little savings: These people are too busy spending their income on "things" and do nothing to prepare for their future. Most of the money they earn is about showing off and pretending to have it all together while they are least prepared for such things like retirement or profitable investments.

These fake rich people could easily live on half their income and save the rest for their retirement or even long term investments. They have poor perspective of money and how it works; their main concern is which neighborhood they live, what car they drive, the closet they have and other unnecessary things that put up the appearance to the society and the fools around who worship them.

Need validation: Fake rich people need you to comment on and care about their things— such as their home, their car, their looks, or their job. They'll often talk about it in a way that prompts questions and discussion. This is their way of validating their own lifestyle choices and they never take positively any constructive criticism to the extent that they can even avoid those who tell them about their fake life.

Own expensive things: The easiest way for a fake rich person to make you think that they are rich is owning expensive things. They lease a nice car or get the newest smart phone to show you. When you see this person with beautiful things, chances are your brain will tell you they have money (at first glance). Gadgets are no longer tools for productivity but material to display fake wealth and net worth.

Fake rich people enjoy showing that they are doing better.
- Better job.

- Fancier car.

- Bigger home.

They won't actually say these things, of course, but they'll drop hints. A fake rich person recently told me their wife

> *It's easier to accumulate wealth if you don't live in a high-status neighborhood.*
> —*Thomas J. Stanley*

Have to dress a specific way: Another easy way to show someone you "have money" is to dress in expensive-looking clothes. A new power suit always makes a person feel important. It's not wrong to dress for success and decent but if you use that as the camouflage for the scarcity and faking to be rich then you are missing the point. You often see women rocking a designer purse, sunglasses, and what seems to be a very expensive outfit and driving an expensive leased car.

What you won't know in the fake rich
Here are some things you may not know about the fake rich:-

Living paycheck-to-paycheck: How can someone making good money keep up with appearances, have a huge home, and buy tons of new material items? They have to spend their money. The fake rich usually are not socking it away in savings they have but many of them are living *paycheck-to-paycheck*. They have very uncertain tomorrow and any tragedy happening in their lives make them quick to take more loans because they do not have emergency funds.

Unhappiness: Although they have beautiful

house, new things all the time, they are unhappy most of the time. They work a ton of hours, and are in a constant vicious cycle of earning and buying; and they are never quite satisfied with stuff. The fake rich always seem to want more in their life as there is unquenchable hunger for materialist things and showing off. These people have to have the newest and best to show others how much money they (think) they have. This causes dissatisfaction on a regular basis and becomes the reason for this perpetual cycle of unhappiness.

Envy others: It takes a strong understanding of people to see this but seeing fake rich people become jealous of you is incredible. Many of fake rich people will laugh at your face if you mention that you are planning to retire at early age. But if you examine their lives, every single one of them leases their car. At one point or another, they're all talking about how tight money is at home. None of them seems to grasp the concept of living below your means. The mindset is that if you can afford the monthly payment, you can afford it. While they're working to pay for new cars, big homes, and material things.

> *Those people whom we define as being wealthy get much more pleasure from owning substantial amounts of appreciable assets than from displaying a high-consumption lifestyle.*
> *– Thomas J. Stanley*

Net worth Calculation

It is a norm in the society and communities for neighbors, co-workers, friends and even family members to compete on what type of car to drive, the neighborhood to live, house to stay in and the school to take your kids regardless of the actual performance of that school so long as it is prestigious. Much money and resources are wasted because of these competitions. If you want to know how you stand financially, consider calculating your real *networth*. In a nutshell, your net worth is everything you own of significance (your assets) minus what you owe in debts (your liabilities). Assets include cash and investments, your home and other real estate, cars or anything else of value you own. *Negative net worth* means that you are living above your means and that shows that you are not ready to retire.

Many people do not have a clue on what is their actual net worth. It's better to have a small house or a car that belongs to you rather than having an expensive house and cars which are on loan or credit. The actual owner is the lender and it is for a fact that the borrower is always a slave to the lender. As a borrower, you know you cannot skip work, payment or change the rules; it is the lender that controls the relationship and your fate. In an unlikely event where the household bread winner passes away, other people cry with pain because the survivors do not know how they will pay the loans and maintain for the lavish lifestyle. In short, most of the individuals are not prepared for rainy days, emergencies and such catastrophes in life and talking about them is taboo.

Among most cultures decent life is considered low income meanwhile showing off, eating out, throwing big parties and fancy dressing without saving for their children has become a noble thing. If you do not invest, it means you want your children to struggle as you did to get to where you are right now. After they leave home, children start life from the very basic level where they do not have any capital. Ideally, our children need to find a solid foundation prepared by parents to build on it. We need to set their foundation and invest on their future for them to leverage. Most parts of the world; relevant education, knowledge and exposure to global issues are so limited. Children in these parts of the world are not prepared to compete at the world platform with all the challenges of globalization. They have a chance to live a better life than us if we prepare them adequately. I strongly believe this is to do justice to the next generation and also to fulfill our obligation as parents.

In many ways, it is not how much one earns annually that counts: It is how one lives each year. It is how much one saves and invests annually that really matters. Thomas Stanley[i] continues to say I am not impressed with what people own. But I'm impressed with what they achieve. I'm proud to be a physician. Always strive to be the best in your field. Don't chase money. If you are the best in your field, money will find you.

Wealthy people teach their children how to talk, to invest and do things. I recently read a book authored by an Accountant, Tom Corley titled, *'Rich Kids: How to Raise Children that Are Happy And Successful[ii]*. When he was working, he used to file the accounts of wealthy people and of other ordinary people. In doing this, he realized that there was a big difference on how wealthy people raise and train their children, so that they also become rich. Poor people have the habit which makes them to remain poor. Tom also observed that poor people were more jealous of other people's success, rude when working with them and unreliable, —simply unpleasant behavior. The wealthy people talk nicely, friendly, courteous and you would always like to be around to them. One key factor to break the poverty circle is to focus on your vision. Dr. Wayne W. Dyer[iii] said if you change the way look at things; things you look at will change. Otherwise, your perspective determines your observation to the environment surrounding you. Then you will start to behave differently, you won't waste time at idle corners, you won't watch TV for long periods of time. Once you start to change the direction, the first observation will be your friends that you used to hang out with; they will start missing you and even bad mouthing you.

We have firsthand experience with that as it happened to us when we followed that path to pursue our dreams and set clear goals to start a university and a home health care agency. The task was so daunting and demanded lots of hours of work away from friends and acquaintances; we were neither on the public eye nor social setups for some time. Guess what; most of our close friends and relatives were very critical and hard on us because of that. However, we remained focused until our goals were completely achieved. I do not advocate for antisocial behavior but if social interactions distract you from accomplishing your goals of breaking the poverty cycle then be it; probably it is time to consider different network of people who add value to your life. Losing focus will make you retire broke, live an artificial life that imitates the rich but actually fake and empty.

Time is Money

I am sure you have heard of the phrase "time is money". While time is a resource that can't be recovered (unlike money) time acts in a lot of ways like money and it should be managed the same way. Think of time as a currency you have and there is two ways of using it: *You spend it or you invest it*—.The question to ask ourselves in how do we use it? Do we spend our time or do we invest it? To hone our time management skills, I want us to start looking at time a little differently. Just like money, in order to get your personal finances in order you have to know first where your money is going. That's why you have to track your expenses. Once you have a list of your common expenses, you eliminate unnecessary purchases and find cheaper alternatives for goods. The difference between income and your adjusted expenses leaves you with money in your pocket that you can invest for profit. You can do exactly the same thing with time; first you have track how you spend your time. Once you know how you use it, that's when you can start working out how to improve your time management. By eliminating some of your time wasters, you can redirect that time to your goals or invest it into something else. One of the adjustments you have to make is that the majority of your time is in alignment with your goals. That is really when you are being productive. Another way of being productive is by using that free time to invest on yourself.

There are certain assets that make up a *"person's net worth"* meaning that they make a person more valuable. Here are some of the assets that are important:

- *Relationships*— your people network and access to people (who you know and who knows you)

- *Knowledge*— in possession of and having access to information (What do you know that is valuable).

- *Money*— the currency that can be traded for many different things (How much do you have and what can you bring on the table).

- *Skills*— specific things you can do really well.

- *Reputation*— your perceived image and status (What do people think honestly about you.

- *Agility*— the flexibility in your life and how well you can adjust to changes.

- *Availability* – the resource you want to have control over the most is your time to do what is necessary.

Working on any of these assets is a great way of

investing your time. That could mean reading more books (knowledge), networking with influential people (relationships), attending a workshop (skills), and so on.

Paradigm Shift
This is exactly how you should look at your time; it is your most valuable resource. Look for ways to cutback on time wasters and start looking for ways to invest your time. This new way of looking at time requires you to make a mental shift of how you look at this precious resource. In order to make this new mind shift work for you, you must be willing to accept that the long-term is more beneficial to you than the short-term. What is interesting is that oftentimes the benefits of each are exactly the opposite. Let's take fast food as an example. In the short-term, it is gratifying to eat that big juicy burger just to tame your hunger and satisfy your taste buds. But in the long run, if you keep eating it often, it is not that beneficial to your health. On the other hand, eating vegetables might not be the most exciting thing in the world in the short-term but the long-term benefits is that you will live healthier. So the short-term benefits are often exactly the opposite of the long-term benefits. The challenge is finding a balance between the two.

You can apply this concept to how you use your time. Are you surrendering yourself to the short-term benefits all the time? Or are you putting in the time to work on what will be beneficial for you in the long run? In other words, are you investing in your time? I am not saying that you should be a workaholic and never have any downtime. Not at all, you need to have balance. What I would like you to see is that you can make that mind shift of using your time without any awareness to the idea of that you can invest your time for long-term benefits. The delay of gratification can be really hard to resist. I know. I sometimes can't resist the urge to go out socializing and partying while knowingly I shouldn't be. But if you want to achieve your big goals, you have to make sacrifices. Like many of successful people and great achievers say, you must be *willing to pay the price of success.* You must be willing to say no to things, suck it up, put in your time and reap the benefits later. The sooner you start investing, the more time is on your side. It is just like investing in assets that provide you interest. By starting early, the compounding effects have much more time for you to take advantage of. If you keep reinvesting some of your time in additional gains in your capacity to act, you can theoretically have a compounding effect with the value of your time (rather than time itself). Just like investing currency, the earlier you start this process, and continue to invest in your capacity, the more time your capacity has to compound, and the greater outcomes you can produce during your lifetime. If you don't pay attention to how you manage your time, it will be spent one way or another. Without any awareness you will end up wondering where it went and complain you need more. Start managing your time and be willing to take the long haul.

Talk is Cheap—Get Results!
Many individuals incline to verbalize opinions, stances, or other traits and subsequent reluctant

to act upon said traits. This is one of the major problems that many people have in connection to actual things that matter most in life such as pursuits to education, financial freedom, physical health and fitness, relationship and behavioral adjustments. Bill Parcells[iv] is the NFL's toughest coach since Vince Lombardi. He use to tell his players regularly and adopted this expression, *'Don't tell me about the labor pain, show me the baby'*. Setting goals gives us something to strive towards and boosts our self-confidence each time we achieve them. More often than not, we are guilty of setting goals that we sometimes fail to meet. I have observed the following to be the major reasons we sometimes fail to meet goals we set for ourselves says Yvonne Kariba[v].

There are 10 reasons why we fail to achieve our goals she continues:-

Excuses, Excuses, Excuses—We all make them! These are often easier to come up with than reasons why we need to do something. They can range from not having enough time to the stars not being correctly aligned. Whatever the case, they paralyze us. Brian Tracy, the world renowned motivational speakers and self-help coach says a disease is called "Excusitis". It can also present itself as *creative avoidance*, an educated way of not doing what we consciously know that it is a priority at that time. I personally come up with mine when I am feeling fearful, anxious, uncertain or just plain old lazy. Sometimes it seems easier and safer not doing anything at all than tackling what needs to be taken care of.

Magnifying our fears more than we do our abilities —Fear of failure has killed so many dreams before they had the chance to take off. We are so accustomed to leaning more towards things not working out than to them working out and often allow this to dissuade us from taking on challenges or setting goals for ourselves.

Fear robs us of our self-confidence and allows us to come up with reasons why we can't do things or make them happen. Grab your fears by the horns and stop underestimating yourself; you are more capable than you think.

Not strong enough "Reasons"— What does your goal mean to you? Why have you set it?

We sometimes chase after things because others expect us to or to keep up with our peers or the "Joneses", if you will. When we set goals for the wrong reasons and chase after things we don't really need or desire; we aren't driven to pursue them, commit to them or achieve them and end up wasting a great deal of time, energy and money that could have been spent pursuing things that resonate with us.

Not setting our priorities right - There are times when I choose to keep up with the Kardashians rather than work on my writing or allow other unimportant things to distract me. It's amazing how we manage to find time for things that don't really add value to our lives, yet give the excuse of lack of time as the reason we can't pursue a goal. It's never ever about having time, but more so about making time. If something is important enough to you, you will find time for it and make it an important enough priority.

Trying your hand at everything—It's so easy to become a Jack of all trades and a master of none. When we spread our attention, energy and focus into many things, we sometimes fail to hone our skills and expertise in the area that we would most flourish in and that is best suited for us. It is important for us to discover what we are really good at, passionate about and most driven to do and focus on and perfect that one thing. We weren't meant to do everything, neither can we do everything.

Crying wolf too often—The more we talk about things we want to do and fail to do them, the more we not only lose creditability with others but mostly with ourselves. When we continually fail to keep our word or meet goals we set, we become demoralized and sometimes lose confidence and faith in ourselves and often times abandon our goals altogether. We need to learn how to walk the walk more than talk the talk and expend our energy into doing things rather than talking about them. As they say, *let the results speak for themselves and your actions do the talking.*

Lacking a plan—When we fail to plan, we plan to fail. A plan is integral in helping us achieve our goals and is a GPS or roadmap that helps get us from point A to B. How do you plan on accomplishing your goal? What actions do you need to take? Outline this and have a clear strategy. Having a plan will give us direction, allows us to better set our priorities as well as ensure we stay on track in the pursuit of our goals. Not having one will have you running around like a chicken without a head and sometimes result in failure.

Lack of commitment—That diet that's started with the very best intentions on Monday but ends that very day as soon as your co-worker walks into the office with a box of donuts. "I don't want to offend her, I'll have just one and start the diet tomorrow", you say. Unless one is fully committed to following through with what one has set to do, reasons and excuses will always pop up that will derail you or cause you to postpone actions you need to take that support your goals

Lack of deadline—Having a deadline forces one to become more focused and disciplined and creates a sense of urgency; factors that keep one driven and attentive to one's goals. When things are open-ended and lack a time frame within which to get accomplished, they sometimes get pushed to the back burner; this often leads to procrastination and at times results in things not getting done at all.

Giving up when the going gets tough—Nothing worth having is ever easy. Some goals will really require our blood, sweat or tears. We live in a time that promotes instant gratification and doesn't encourage perseverance enough and where quitting is often viewed as an option. There is no such thing as over-night success; diligence, dedication and discipline are required if we want to meet our goals or change our lives. We also have to be willing to put in the time and endure long pain in the process.

Areas of Focus
Getting wealthy begins with the way you think and what you *believe about making money* and fi-

nancial freedom, writes Siebold in "How Rich People Think."[vi] The author continues by saying that the rich eventually figures out that training your mind to find solutions to difficult problems is the real secret to making money. The good news is this is possible for anyone who conditions their mind to think this way, and then transforms thought into action. Secondly, successful people *command their thoughts and emotions.* As soon as bad thoughts intrude, they cast out anything that challenges their ability to succeed at the task at hand. They do not dwell on negative notions. Their self-talk is positive and not overly critical. They replace bad thoughts with good ones; they choose to be positive over being negative about possibilities. Because successful people engage in self-improvement daily and are constantly involved in positive things, they don't allow themselves time to indulge in negative emotions. *—Wealth and poverty are both a mindset.*

[i] Thomas J. Stanley, "Stop Acting Rich: And Start Living Like A Real Millionaire". Copyright 2014, ISBN: 0470482559

[ii] Tom Corley, Rich Kids: How to Raise Our Children to Be Happy and Successful, 2nd Edition, Two Harbors Press, Minneapolis MN

[iii] Wayne W. Dyer. "Your Erroneous Zones: Step-by-Step Advice for Escaping the Trap of Negative Thinking and Taking Control of Your Life" Copyright ©1976 ISBN 978-0060919764

[iv] Bill Parcells and Nunyo Demasio, "Parcells: A Football Life" Publisher: Crown Archetype Copyright ©2014

[v] Yvonne Kariba, Contributor, Writer, Blogger & Green Smoothie Lover 10 Reasons We Fail to Achieve Our Goals. https://www.huffpost.com/entry/10-reasons-we-fail-to-ach_b_7152688

[vi] Steve Siebold, How Rich People Think, CreateSpace Independent Publishing Platform, 2013

eight

The Power of Vision and Sight

"If you can imagine it; you can achieve it. If you can dream it, you can become it."
—William Arthur Ward

ometime back I interviewed with a certain prestigious university seeking a position as a medical science professor. As I was preparing myself for this long sought opportunity, two polarizing ideas were racing in mind. Whether I am going to get the job because of my credentials, experience and academic achievements or I would not because I had several unsuccessful interviews before this one. As they say in the south, *"born and bred"*, trained and raised in Tanzania, East Africa and learned another African language as adult in Southern Africa has left me with a characteristic different foreign accent. The fact that I am multilingual and American English is now my fourth language makes me pronounce and annunciate words differently from a native speaker. I struggled with this limit belief for a long time. I'm still taking American accent training courses for people to understand me without difficulties especially my students and my coworkers. Well, I landed this particular job and learned something very interesting from a colleague who happened to be in the search committee and later became a good friend. Though the department was interested in good academic credentials, qualification and experience, they were also seeking to diversify the teaching faculty, and make the institution take an international outlook so they were having a preference in a candidate that has an international experience and spin, lo and behold; I happened to be the person! All those circumstances favored me to get that job and my foreign accent worked for me instead of against me, my challenge and limiting belief in fact became a cutting edge and a competitive advantage to the presented opportunity.

Dreamer's Haven

"If your dream doesn't scare you, it's too small", so says Mark Batterson[i] in his "Chase the Lion". All of us have dreams and aspirations. Sometimes we are just afraid to chase the dream because of what it will cost. Other times, because of life's circumstances, we allow the dream to die. He challenges us to awaken the sleeping dreams within us, give us the faith to chase those dreams, and help us develop new dreams. I personally have always been a dreamer. Since as long as I could remember, I would have these wild fantasies and visions of doing and achieving great things in my life. But I'm not alone in that aspect, I know there are

plenty of dreamers out there. And while society might work to dismiss some of us as pure noise, there are enormous benefits to dreaming often and dreaming big. *Dreaming involves holding tight to a vision of a better life, one of success and abundance.* While getting there might be difficult, having to deal with setbacks and failures along the way, it's surely well worth it.

Anyone who's achieved a big goal knows just how true that statement is. Yet, although some of us might like to dream, we all dream differently. We don't always hold tight to those dreams, knowing that we can and will do anything in our power to make them a reality. *The truth of the matter is that many of us give up on our dreams.* We throw in that proverbial towel when the going gets tough. We give up rather than persist through the torment and pain of another failure. But being a starry-eyed dreamer isn't about giving up. Dreaming often and dreaming big actually provides us with a platform for growth and success. —*It all starts with the dream.* And, while there are plenty of benefits to living a "*normal*" life — one of complacency and compliance executed with a subdued spirit — there's nothing quite like being a *dreamer*, and having wild visions of a life that you know you're destined to live, even if you're not living it today, in this very moment.

How to Dream Big

Children dream big, it is part of their genetic fiber —their overall make-up, if you will. They never think small because they aren't hindered by the standard limitations that hold adults back. If you ask a child what he wants for Christmas, he might say, "I want two swimming pools! One in the back-yard and one in the front". While it's easy to dismiss a child's dreams as being silly or unrealistic, who's to say that's so? Who's to say any of our dreams are silly or unrealistic? Just because something goes against the grain, or runs in the opposite direction of societal norms, it doesn't mean that it's impossible. We can all use a bit of childlike amusement in ourselves. There's absolutely nothing wrong with it. And if your dreams don't scare you, then they're not big enough. The only thing holding you back from achieving them, is yourself. We can be our own worst enemies in so many instances, especially when we don't believe wholeheartedly in ourselves.—*You cannot achieve anything more than you see; all that you see has been given unto you.* So our biggest challenge is to improve our mental sight and capacity to visualization and remove all limiting beliefs that hinder us from rising up and take hold of what we already see inside ourselves.

Limiting Beliefs

Limiting behaviors originate from *limiting beliefs*. Our beliefs form the basis of our experiences and how we perceive ourselves and the world around us. When our beliefs are limited, we limit our perception and experience of what is possible. It doesn't matter if those beliefs are false. As long as we believe them, they will accordingly impact and mold our perception of experience. The more limiting our beliefs, the less powerful we feel. A belief is a conviction or generalization that is accepted as truth without positive proof or knowledge.

- A *limiting belief* is one that places artificial boundaries around your personal potential. Some of the symptoms of the limit beliefs in our lives include but not limited to:-

- *Inability* to taking risks and daring big things outside our comfort zone.

- *Stagnation* that keeps us where we are and never make attempts to progress in our career or life.

- *Obstruction* to growth and robs our self-confidence, self-esteem and self-initiative.

- *Lack of Breakthrough* that keeps us repeating negative patterns and makes us go through a vicious cycle of failure and lack of desirable results.

- *Lack of Accountability* that prevents us from taking responsibility for our life and shift blames to somebody else.

- *Fear of the Unknown (Xenophobia)* fills doubt and fear for things that are unsubstantiated prevents us from going after our dreams. It makes us give good reasons and excuses for why it is not going to work and for not doing what we really want to do.

- *Failure to Thrive* that feeds on procrastination and provides creative avoidance.

- *Defeatist Pessimism* prompts us to find *"evidence"* to support negative behavior and thought patterns that result in lack of achievement. Failure to imagining the possibilities and makes us focus on impossibilities or the negative side of things.This is when we gravitate more on Murphy's Law that states *"anything that can go wrong will go wrong"*.

Common Limiting Beliefs
- *I don't have this skill.*

- *I'm not good at this.*

- *Others can do it better than me.*

- *I'm not smart enough*

- *I have a wrong skin color*

- *I have a funny accent*

- *I'm not experienced enough.*

- *I'm not smart enough.*

- *I'm not important enough.*

- *I'm too young or I'm too old.*

- *I don't have the money.*

- *I don't have the time.*

- *It's just not in my genes.*

- *It's too hard.*

- *I don't deserve success; it's for others.*

- *I was born like that; I can't change.*

- *My background works against me*

- *Nothing ever works out for me.*

- *Nobody ever notices the work I do.*

- *I never get what I want.*

- *People normally hate me for no reason.*

- *This is just "the way it is."*

- *I have no control over this.*

- *I have nothing to offer.*

- *It runs in our family!*

Most of the time, such beliefs exist beneath the surface, in our subconscious mind, and have been there for years and years (usually since childhood). We might not even know they exist—but most of us have at least a few.

Overcoming Limiting Belief

Most of us have beliefs which limit us in some ways, impoverishing our lives and preventing us from achieving our true potential. Here's how to overcome these and so enable and empower your life and those of others.

Isolate the belief: First consider the belief that is limiting you. Many of us make limiting choices without realizing that they are based on flawed, limiting beliefs. Find times where you have done something (or not done something) that seemed to limit you in some way. Then ask 'What beliefs led to this choice?' Keep digging, asking 'What belief underlies that belief?' until you come to the limiting belief or beliefs. Also consider what concerns or frightens you and so limits you. What do you fear? Why? What beliefs lead you to such fears?

Seek the source: Think back to when you first had the belief. When did you first belief this? What happened for you to believe it? Were you told to believe it by someone? Was it a parent, teacher, or maybe someone who was not thinking kindly about you? Was it based on an experience? Did you try something once, failed and then formed the belief that you were incapable? Or that 'other people' think in certain ways?

Recognize the falsehood: In doing the above steps, you may already realize that the limiting belief is just that: a belief which is both limited and limiting. You are holding it because you were told to or because it helped you once. Take time to reflect on this and recognize the full extent of the belief, how false it really is and especially how it has limited you in the past. Feel free to get angry about this. In doing this, you may need to accept that you are not perfect, which can be disconcerting (beware of limiting beliefs here also). You must be open to learning and ready to change.

Form empowering beliefs: When you want to change a belief, you may well need an enabling belief which will replace the old one. Be careful with these, making them realistic and not setting yourself up for disappointment. It can be more effective, for example, to believe that you can do public speaking than to immediately believe you are world-class at it. If you lack a skill that needs to be learned, believing you now have it is likely to lead to problems. It is better to believe you are able to learn (which is one of the most empowering beliefs you can have). Believing *'I can'* can be more powerful than thinking *'I am'*. In a similar vein, if you thought yourself stupid, notice the different between thinking you are not stupid as opposed to being intelligent. There is a difference between 'Not A' and 'B', both of which may initially seem to be the opposite of 'A'. The trick is to consider where the belief will take you, what will it let you think and do, and what evidence will it create, as in the next step.

Start 'as if': A good starting point for many beliefs is to act as if the belief were true. Just pretend you are an actor and are going through the motions. Your mind is not great at knowing when you are acting or not, with the result that what you do will steadily become what you believe. One reason for this is the way the consistency principle works. This is a classic way that brainwashing works. All you are doing, is brainwashing yourself into the beliefs that will serve you best.

Create evidence of success: The most powerful and unshakeable beliefs are those that are based on lots of evidence. So now you have recognized and challenged your limiting beliefs and found empowering beliefs, then you need to start creating evidence. Depending on what it is, you may be more sensible to start small. If you believed that you could not talk with strangers, try starting with simple politeness, saying 'thank you' and 'after you', which immediately show that actually you can talk to strangers. Then build up with brief small-talk, such as about the weather or sports. When you see a success, no matter how small, use this as an affirmation. Tell yourself *'I did it!'* and reflect on how you are now a changed person, with no way back. When you have done something new, it cannot be undone. Keep building evidence until the limiting belief seems daft and you are now comfortable in your new belief. Determination and persistence are critical in this. Also watch for other limiting beliefs which get in the way (change these too if you need to).

Small Business Owner

As our college grew and classroom space became a challenge for our students, staff and faculty, we decided to launch in acquiring a bigger campus that was available for sale two blocks away. The need was so obvious since some of the faculty was depressed most of the time. They were demoralized as the working environment was lowering their efficiency and excitement to work. We sought commercial mortgage from different financial institutions including our own bank to no avail. All banks turned our application down because of our small cash flow and did not believe we will be able to service the loan. This confirmed our limiting belief that we are small a business minority owned business and nobody can ever believe our story. We did not give up! We moved from one bank to the other until we finished all in the city. The seller surprised us by telling us that they decided to finance us for 5 years. They looked at all the applications and their board of trustees thought that since we had an identical vision with the founders and original owners of the campus building, we were the best candidate to get the facility but if they don't give us the loan, no financial institute would because of our cash flow. They chose to finance us because our vision was coinciding with their vision. The *limiting belief* that we had was since we are a small business; neither financial institution nor seller would finance our vision. I believe most of us have many incidences like these that what you think would work against us ends up working for us. Learn to journal all those incidences to boost your confidence to counter all negative and limiting beliefs in your life.

Success in Helping Others

Without a doubt, the fastest way to achieve success is to first help others succeed. Yet, there seems to be a belief in the business and social world that the only way to get ahead is to only watch out for 'number one'. That is simply not the case. Brian Tracy explained it best when he said, "Successful people are always looking for opportunities to help others. Unsuccessful people are always asking, 'What's in it for me?'" The fact is that our greatest successes in life often come through helping others to succeed, and without question, when you focus on helping others succeed your eventual payoff will always be far greater than your investment. Here are five ways that everyone can help others to succeed, and in turn find greater success themselves:-

Take interest in the details of other people's lives.

When you make the effort in to remember the important details of others' lives, such as their spouse's name, their children, their hobbies, etc. your ability to be a positive impact in their life increases tremendously. It lets the other person know how important they are to you. It lets them know that you truly care about their life. The more a person knows that you genuinely care about them, the more they will in turn move heaven and earth to help you with the things you want. And with the contact tracking tools available on our electronic devices today, it is incredibly simple to make quick notes about people so your memory can always be fresh.

Point people in the right direction:

Sharing your network freely with others and be willing to introduce people to others you know who can help advance or forward their goals. When you have a networking event to attend, invite people to come with you that could benefit from expanding their network as well. The more you open up your network to others, the more you will find your own network expanding, and you might just be amazed at the incredible contacts you end up receiving from the most unlikely people.

Inspiring people

This is worth far more than motivating a person. You can motivate an employee with a raise, or a fancy title, and for a period of time they will feel motivated to work harder to show their appreciation. But after a little time passes they begin to forget the additional money and the fancier title because those have now become the "norm" and you'll find that, once again, they are back to needing added motivation to take their performance to the next level. On the other hand if you inspire an employee by treating them with respect and frequently letting them know, in a sincere way, just how much you appreciate them and the contribution they are making, you will find that they are constantly motivated to continually increase their efforts on an ongoing basis. Inspiring others is the ultimate form of perpetual motivation.

Give honest feedback

It has to done in a respectful and constructive way, this is one of the most difficult things for people to learn to do well. Many people don't like confronting issues and would rather dance around them, while those who do like confrontation often aren't respectful or constructive in the way they give it. But those who can learn the skill of giving honest and open feedback in a constructive and uplifting way can have a tremendous impact on improving the lives of others. One trick that has helped me with giving good feedback is to always make sure that I am walking into the conversation with the mindset of truly caring about this person and wanting to genuinely help them to improve. If I go into the conversation with that motivation then my words naturally come out better. The more you give feedback to help others improve, the more you will find that they will, in turn, open up to you and give you feedback that helps you to improve as well.

Others' needs come first

You have to be willing to put the needs of others first, even when it means you have to overlook your own wants.

> *"Marine leaders are expected to eat last because the true price of leadership is the willingness to place the needs of others above your own."*
> —*Simon Sinek.*

This particular point can be one of the most intimidating things to actually do because in the moment it feels so counterintuitive to put others' needs above your own when doing so appears to require you to set aside your own desires. But as counterintuitive as it sounds, the fact is that it genuinely works. Perhaps not instantly, but over time it eventually leads to getting you everything you want and more. I can say this with absolute conviction because I have seen it in my own life. As a CEO I found that the more I focused on helping my employees to personally succeed both in their professional and personal lives, the more my entire company succeeded —and as a result, I personally succeeded far more than I ever would have imagined.

World Platform

While there are many different ways that one can work towards becoming successful, one theme will remain true throughout nearly every single avenue one chooses, and that is:

> *Our success is determined by how many people we are able to help solve a problem, or helping others to improve the level and quality of something in their life.*

From the very early beginnings of life, through our recent industrial and population booms, this has been a true tenet of life. This can date backwards from the most successful hunters of the tribe and community in early history, to Andrew Carnegie figuring out how to make a better product in a scalable way to help America; and to recently the late Steve Jobs of *Apple* and Elon Musk of *Tesla Motors*. With their technological revolutions, those who have been successful have all helped others solve one or more problems, and often in big ways. Why is the world set up this way, and how can you scale your idea to do the same? The emphasis here is to see how you too, can achieve success through a focus on serving and helping others. As Gary Vee says, "The reason I put my best out there for free, is because most of you won't take action on it."

You are unique in your skills and tool set. No one else in the world has your unique experiences and views on things. Just look at how Apple Inc., tanked in the time that Steve Jobs had been forced out, and how dominant it was, once again, upon his return. He understood what people needed, and how to help them – even if they didn't yet know it! Remember, only you have special skills and views to share with the world. When you go out and share it with the intention of helping others improve their lives, the abundance of the universe will begin to flow to you. *This is the universal principle of life that those who water others will themselves be watered.* Perhaps it is because of the seemingly interwoven concept of life. That each of our lives, are more connected than we realize. If we think of the *"Six degrees of Separation Theory"*, it states that we are all just a few people away from other[ii].So when we share a skill or ability that we have to help others improve their life or situation, word gets out. You quickly become an important part of the community.

Let's take a look at the world of sports, specifically Magic Johnson, one of the best players to ever play the game of basketball. The thing made Earving "Magic" Johnson so unique as a player, was his realization that by focusing on learning about his *teammates*—and how he could make them better –he was able not only to win more, but have more fun and help them play better as well. The problem the world faces now, more so than the 1980's when Magic began playing, is the *"Me Syndrome"*. The *Me Syndrome* can be very devastating to what would otherwise be great teams and world class companies. Especially nowadays, as the proliferation of "1-person startups" and automation are becoming much more widespread, we see this "Me First" mentality and epidemic throughout the world.

While many people wish to be millionaires, to become these huge successes, they fail to recognize one of the very basic tenets of how one is able to leverage their skills, talents or ideas in order to become that success. In other words *package your gift in a way that you can help as many people as possible; and afford others the opportunity to bring their unique skills and abilities to help you as well.*

Connecting with other human beings and showing that we have skills and tools to help them is an incredibly important part of the road to success —no matter what the field. One of the greatest parts of being human is the incredibly far-reaching connections that we can have with others. As the "The six degree of separation theory" shows, our 'human resources' reach out much farther than we could imagine – yet so few of us actually take advantage of this.

Here's an example from the movies (based on a real story): "The Pursuit of Happyness" with Will Smith. The main character has bought into the bone scanner business in the 70's. He has to rely on selling one of these 100 machines to a relatively small group of doctors in the San Francisco region. When he does sell a machine, he has money for the next six weeks. But if he doesn't sell one, he starves. Realizing that he must find another way to support himself and his son (as the bone scanners are hard to sell), he starts working at the investment firm Dean Witter, helping others make more money by investing wisely. What I love about this story is not just that he changed *his mindset in order to help others, but that he hustled to help others.* He was in early, having to figure out how to be the best in his class, while having to leave 3 hours earlier than his classmates, so he could pick up his son.

This has been the idea behind many successful ventures in the history of man from the — Model T to the smartphone. These inventions didn't make the inventors money because they sold them for excessive amounts to just a select few people. They produced and sold them to help more and more folks improve their quality of life. It's one of the rules of the universe: the more abundance and value you provide to more people, even more abundance will be returned to you.

> *"Give, and you will receive. Your gift will return to you in full—pressed down, shaken together to make room for more, running over, and poured into your lap. The amount you give will determine the amount you get back."*
>
> —*Dr. Luke, The Physician 6:38*

As Pat Reilly says in his book "The Winner Within", all of us are team players, whether we know it or not. Our significance arrives through our vital connections to other people, through all the teams in our lives[iii]. Family life is a central team experience. Career teams may be a fledgling company or a department in a very large corporation, an industry leader or a struggling contender, a team of scientists or doctors, or the faculty of a school. A neighborhood community action group is a team, and so is a congregation. You can be the one who lifts it, who sets the stage for its greatest accomplishments. That is what will make you great. The complex inner rhythms of teamwork —flows of ambition, power, cooperation, and emotion – are the keys to making dreams come true."So what are you waiting for? Get out there and start helping others. Serve them to the absolute best of your abilities, as you build your new team to success.

In a heated group discussion with our family friend, his wife said innocently—*"I wish and pray to have enough money in order to give it to charity and start making a difference in other people's lives"*. My response was simple and straightforward that the way one uses the money now is a reflection of his or her life philosophy pertaining to core values and priority. Money is never enough; the more you have the more needs and demands come with it. The way we use our $3000 monthly salary today will reflect exactly how we will use the $300,000 and the $3 million that we are going to have in future. It's better to start exercising and flexing those giving and charity muscles now than later when it hurts most.

My wife ambushed me with a mind bogging question one night after putting our little kids to bed. She asked me, "if you find yourself having unexpectedly $10 million dollars in your account, how will you use it?" I was quick to respond with all confidence and pride, I answered with anticipation and joyful of heart glittering through my little eyes and said, *"I will spend it exactly how I currently do with my salary!"*The way you spend your salary now is exactly how you will spend much of the big sums of money once they come your way. If you budget and spend on things like tithing, expenses, helping others, education, investment, vacation and fun, you will do exactly that when you get lots of money and the only difference will be the amounts.

"You are where you are and what you are because of yourself", says Brian Tracy[iv] in his book "Million Dollar habits". Everything you are today, or ever will be in the future, is up to you. Your life today is the sum total result of your choices, decisions and actions up to this point. You can create your own future by changing your behaviors. You can make new choices and decisions that are more consistent with the person you want to be and the things you want to accomplish with your life.

[i] Mark Batterson, Chase the Lion: If your dream doesn't scare you; it's too small. Copyright © 2016, Multnomah Inc

[ii] Six Degree of Separation Theory https://whatis.techtarget.com/definition/six-degrees-of-separation

[iii] Pat Riley "The Winner Within" A Life Plan For Team Players, Paperback, ISBN 9780425141755, Copyright ©1994

[iv] Brian Tracy, Million Dollar Habits: Practical, Proven, Power Practices to Double and Triple Your Income Copyright ©2004 by Entrepreneur Media Inc. ISBN 1-932156-70-4

Other Books

Spouse as a Partner: *How to work together as teammates in Business, Ministry and Other Projects.*

Authors: 1. Dr. Lucas D. Shallua
           2. Dr. Dorothy E. Shallua

Commercialize Your Gifts and Abilities: *How to Profit from your Talents, Skills and Passions and Never be Poor Again*

Author: Dr. Lucas D. Shallua

Finish Line: *The Art of Starting, Executing and Finishing Life Assignments and Mission.*

Author: Dr. Lucas D. Shallua

www.ingramcontent.com/pod-product-compliance
Lightning Source LLC
Chambersburg PA
CBHW031544040426
42452CB00006B/173